Pain as a Portal

Pain as a Portal

A Philosophy to Explore Your Potential

APRIL SIMONE

First published by The Kind Press in 2025
thekindpress.com

Copyright © April Simone 2025
All rights reserved. No part of this publication may be reproduced without prior written permission from the publisher.

We at The Kind Press acknowledge that Aboriginal and Torres Strait Islander peoples are the Traditional Custodians and the first storytellers of the lands on which we live and work; and we pay our respects to Elders past and present.

A catalogue record for this book is available from the National Library of Australia.
ISBN: 9781763508392 (paperback)

Artwork and cover image by April Simone
Author photo by Ella Ellington, Biomi Photo
Typeset by Nicola Matthews, Nikki Jane Design

DISCLAIMER: The information contained in this book is based on personal experiences and insights and is provided for inspiration and informational purposes only. It is not intended to be, nor should it be used as, a substitute for professional diagnosis, advice, or treatment of any mental illness. To the maximum extent permitted by applicable law, the publisher and author disclaim all liability for any loss or harm arising from the use of this book or reliance on its content. Readers are encouraged to seek appropriate professional guidance for their individual circumstances. Additionally, some names, locations and identifying characteristics of individuals in this book have been changed to protect the privacy of those depicted.

to the pain,
for being my portal
to *delight*

CONTENTS

A note from the author	xi
Introduction	xii
Initial contemplations	xiii
The intention of Pain as a Portal	xiv
Overview of how humans experience pain	xvi

Part I
METTĀMORPHOSIS

PHASES OF A BUTTERFLY AND ANALOGICAL COMPARISONS	7
Phase 1	8
Phase 2	8
Phase 3	9
Phase 4	12
THE CYCLE	15
IMPLEMENTING THE PAIN PROCESS	17
THE PAIN PROCESS	18
Phase 1	19
Phase 2	21
Phase 3	26
Phase 4	39
PLEASURE AS A PORTAL	44
THE DIFFERENCE BETWEEN SELF-SOOTHING, I.C.E AND SELF-CARE	45
DIAMOND METTĀMORPHOSIS TEMPLATE	46
FUTURE PORTALS	48

Part II
CASE STUDIES
54

Part III
MY PORTALS

confusion
as a portal to
gratitude
71

hopeless
as a portal to
hopeful
83

empathy
as a portal to
compassion
101

violated
as a portal to
forgiveness
109

insecure
as a portal to
love
123

grief
as a portal to
soul connection
135

misunderstood
as a portal to
liberation
145

questions
as a portal to
knowing
155

pleasure
as a portal to
!!!
167

all of my pleasure and pain
as a portal to
this book
173

An Honouring	*189*
Unwavering Gratitude	*191*
Closing Note	*195*
Tribute To Works Of Art	*197*
About The Author	*200*

A note from the author

This book will speak to the many aspects of pain and suffering that humans experience, along with some of my own personal experiences. As the contents of this book may invoke a sense of pain into your experience, you are required to take radical self-responsibility moving forward. You can do this by reminding yourself that you are a sovereign being and independent thought is not only welcomed but encouraged. If something does not feel true to your core being, use your discernment and allow it to move past you like a gust of wind.

Each chapter ends with the following symbol: ❀

This serves as a visual reminder that as you read and contemplate the words and concepts in *Pain as a Portal*, to do so with loving-kindness towards yourself. This may look like regularly asking your body what it needs, which may look like sipping a cup of tea, taking a break, going for a walk, smelling a flower, taking a deep inhale and exhale, or by closing the book.

If pain is ignited, I do hope that you can continue to move through and at least finish part one, so that the mind and body finds some closure and suggestions of tools of how to lovingly tend to the pain. If the pain invoked feels too large to move through alone, I encourage you to reach out to a trusted person, doctor or allied health professional for support. Sometimes asking for and accepting support is the most radical form of self-help.

Introduction

I am April, born on and currently residing on Anaiwan Country, New South Wales, Australia, where the gum leaves rustle in multi-climate winds and earth wisdom is an unconditionally loving friend.

I have always been filled with wonder and curiosity about all aspects of the human experience. The area that takes the strongest hold of my heart is humans and their behaviours, pain, suffering and the purpose of life as a sentient being. This has led me down the many paths of service in various community service sectors. For the moment though, home is in my private practice where I guide children, teenagers and adults through their pain with intentional creative expression. I use the modalities of Sandplay Therapy, Art Therapy, Dancing Freedom (to name my favourites) and now, the 'Pain *as a* Portal' model.

Throughout the pages, you will come to know me quite well, so without further ado, I send you reverence and love while you ponder the upcoming.

Thank you for spending your time with me.

Initial contemplations

The human experience provides us with everything we need to experience love, joy, and fulfillment. While our accessibility to water, food, shelter and money varies significantly across the globe, there is one thing that we all have in common, no matter who we are. That thing is abundant access to *pain*. While we are alive in this human form, pain will be part of our experience. My idealistic nature and desire for infinite peace squirms at this reality.

I have certainly met with the many depths and faces of pain. It has been through these meetings and a deep longing to understand *why* suffering is part of this life, that I have come to live in service to befri*end* my pain. Through doing this, I have discovered that pain serves as a portal, a pathway, or a doorway to an abundance of gifts that come in many unexpected forms.

Through curious inquiry it became apparent that all along there was a sequence that all of my pains followed. By playing with, trusting and embodying this sequence, all aspects of my life have changed for the better. This includes how I experience my day-to-day life, how I experience pain, how I guide the people I work with and how I interact with all living beings. It has softened me and made me hopeful. It is teaching me patience and trust. It has led me to a new understanding of love. It has freed me from extended periods of suffering and attachments that I have held in my body and spirit. I am bursting with excitement to share this with you.

The intention of Pain as a Portal

My intention is for this transmission to serve as a guide, to travel alongside you on your journey to discover the many gifts that your pain has to offer.

> Part One, explores the model of Pain as a Portal which includes the philosophy behind it and a step-by-step guide on how to frame, process and morph your pain into a gift.
>
> Part Two, offers case studies to provide a clear example of how I have incorporated this model into my life.
>
> In Part Three, I share personal stories in a narrative style of writing, to offer myself to you from a place of vulnerability and as sustenance of hope for your mind and heart.

I have aimed to present the contents in a way that hopefully, most can understand and implement, as the process outlined can be used by people of all ages. I have left out the complex science to aid this aim. If you enjoy the science of concepts or their psychological benefit, you can find a reference to some works that have inspired me towards the end of the book, or I encourage you to undertake some of your own research.

Whether this transmission resonates with you or not, I give thanks, as either way I believe that both outcomes lead you closer to your essence. I am not asking for your belief in this process.

Belief lives in the mind and what I am asking you to contemplate is beyond a matter of the mind. This message is directed at your heart and soul, where remembrance, truth and knowing resides. I ask you to look beyond what I am saying and listen to your own heart. May it serve as a homecoming of your innate inner knowing that you are exactly where you are meant to be, and your existence is a gift to this world.

Overview of how humans experience pain

Pain serves as a messenger, in response to an experience. Pain requests our mind's attention, so that we can take intentional action moving forward. This concept is part of the field of affective neuroscience. Each type of pain holds many messages. It takes getting to know the pain with curiosity, to better understand what message it has for you.

Pain is a subjective experience. Each type of pain can be experienced in isolation or simultaneously with other types of pain.

Physical pain can be felt in a singular body part or multiple parts simultaneously. The body produces chemicals that send a message to the brain to get its attention. Physical pain can be described as a dull, achy, stabbing, sharp, shooting, burning or a numb sensation. These messages might be telling you not to touch a hot stove or that your body has an illness that needs attention.

Emotion is the experience of energy moving through the body. This is generally felt as sensations of contraction or expansion.

Emotional pain is when the body experiences a contraction of sensation, which feels physically unpleasant to the body. The brain then labels this sensation as an *unpleasant feeling* such as guilt, shame, anger, sadness, loneliness, despair, anxiety or fear. These messages might be asking you to question whether you are required to make a change. For example, say you feel fear regularly in a relationship. What might the fear want you to do, to show your body that you care about it?

Emotional pleasure is the expansion of sensations which feels physically pleasant to the body. The brain then labels this sensation as a *pleasant feeling* such as joy, love, gratitude, freedom and excitement, to name a few. For example, say you feel joy regularly in a relationship. What might the joy be telling you about this relationship?

Mental or psychological pain is when the mind perceives pain within its thoughts, concepts and perceptions. Some examples include a discrepancy between the ideal and actual perception of self, feeling separate to others or the self, inadequacy, emptiness or a 'spiralling' sensation in the mind.

Suffering is experienced when you feel trapped or stuck within or with a pain. It will often have a complex concept or story attached to it, that you may be unsure how to move beyond.

Trauma in Greek means *wound*. Trauma can occur within the body as a response to a single experience, repeated experiences or varied experiences where the mind and body experiences unsafety and harm. A constellation of long-lasting and complex pains, are lodged in the body, mind and nervous system, lasting long past the originating experience/s. This creates chronic constraints to your relationship with yourself and the world.

IMPORTANT NOTE

As pain serves as a messenger, it similarly also serves as a portal or doorway to a gift or many. We will explore this in depth in the upcoming chapters. I want to ascertain that the *pain,* which has been in *response* to an experience, is the portal in the model in this book.

Some experiences that cause pain are utterly despicable and by no means acceptable. I am talking especially about experiences that fall under the term 'abuse' which includes physical, verbal, sexual, psychological, financial, emotional abuse and neglect. The Pain *as a* Portal method does not condone or excuse these experiences.

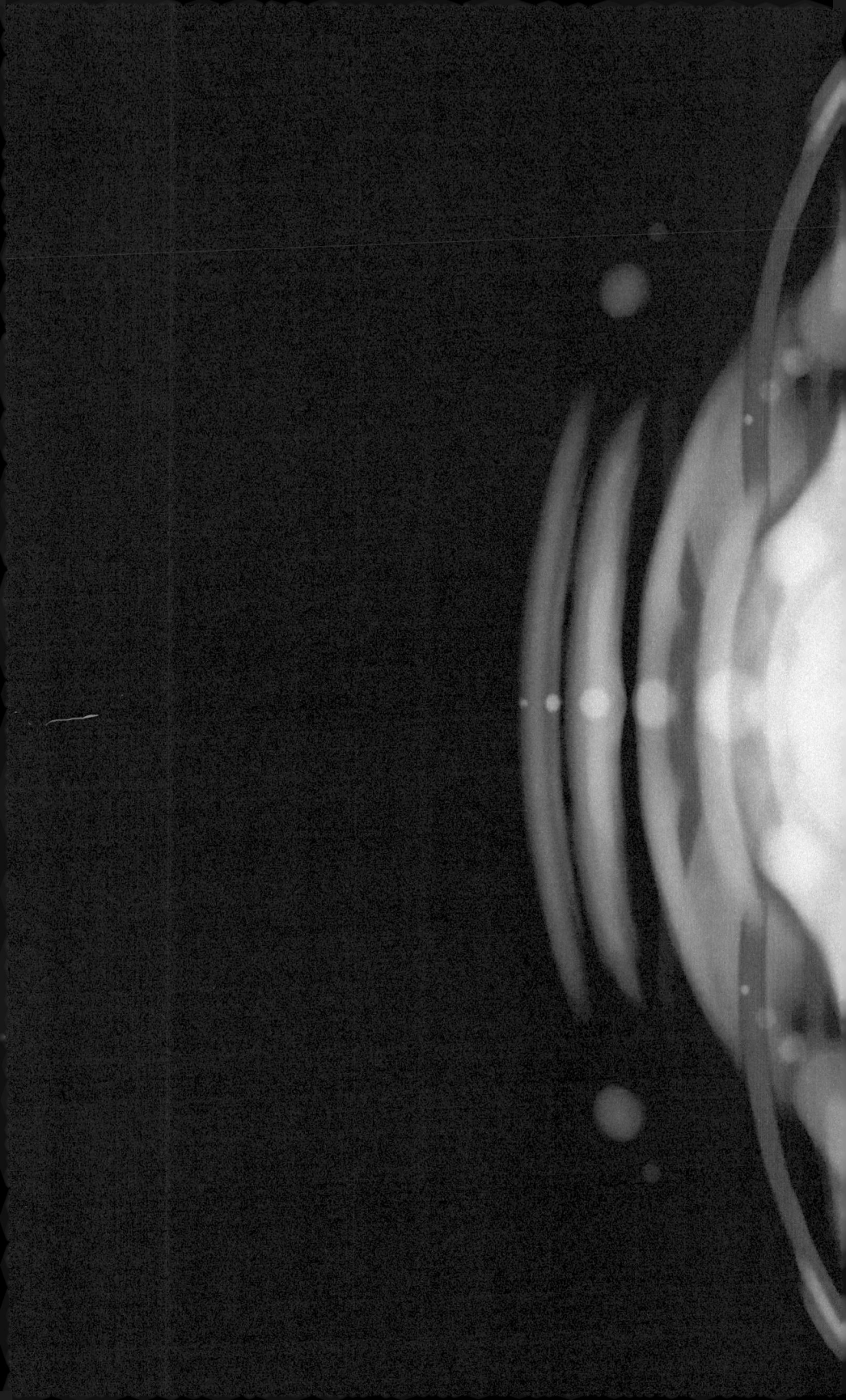

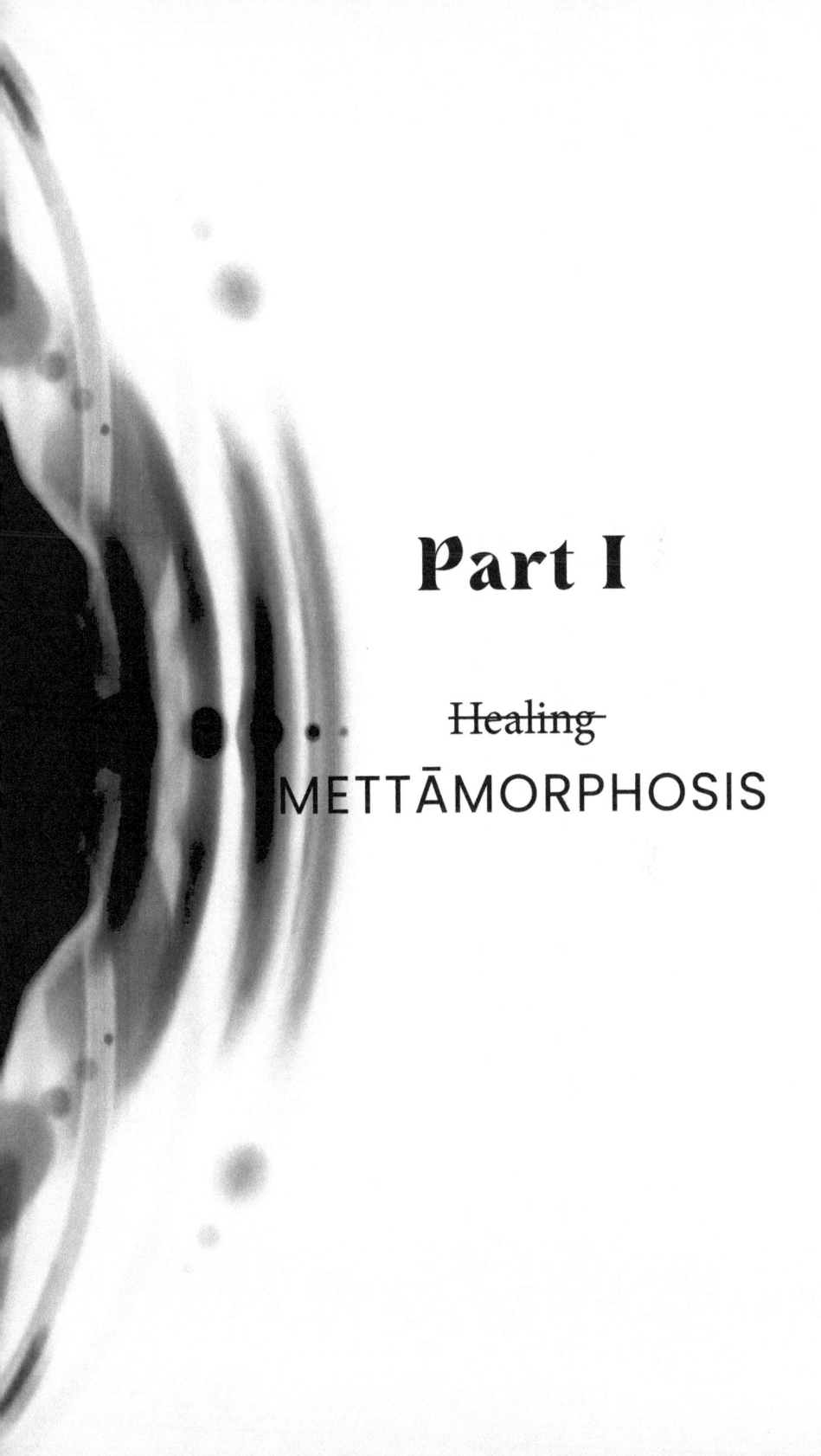

Part I

~~Healing~~
METTĀMORPHOSIS

One of my favourite aspects of being human is experiencing or witnessing compassion. In my mid 20s, I learned the teachings of mettā and mettā meditation and I knew I had found one of my true loves.

> ✦ **mettā** *(noun)*
>
> *unconditional love and loving-kindness, benevolence, and amity*

Mettā meditation, or often loving-kindness meditation, is the practice of cultivating mettā. It generally consists of silent repetitions of phrases to oneself such as 'May you be happy' or 'May you be free from suffering'. The practice gradually increases in difficulty with respect to the targets that receive the practitioner's compassion or loving-kindness. At first, the practitioner is targeting oneself, then loved ones, neutral ones, difficult ones and finally all beings.

Through much experimentation, I have come to know and feel that when we bring compassion and loving-kindness into our moments with others and especially ourselves, we enter into a completely different realm of experience. By choosing to embody compassion, we are choosing to enter into love, joy, humility, peace and forgiveness—some of life's most precious gifts.

Practicing Mettā didn't just bring joy and rainbows, it was hard at times, as it challenged a lot of my conditioned thinking and belief systems. For example, I wanted to hold onto anger towards certain people, as it felt like they deserved my anger. What I eventually learnt though, was that holding onto anger only hurt me. The anger offered many messages and lessons, but ultimately required me to let it go.

In 2022, I learned about how the words we use, can affect us physiologically and psychologically. I began practicing being intentional with the words that I used. I suddenly became hypersensitive to the word 'healing' and the societal goal for all to be on 'the path to healing'. This was a concept that I have loved for years, and it suddenly initiated physical, emotional and spiritual discomfort in my body. My mind and body were hearing that the desired destination was to be 'healed' which led me to look up its definition.

✦ **heal** (verb)

to become sound, healthy or whole again

Most of my favourite teachers in the self-help and spiritual development field use this term in a wholesome and loving manner but when I asked my body how it felt when I told it, *You need to be found to be sound again, you need to be whole again*, it responded with tender pain. I judged myself for my pain and I felt less than the wise teachers, which fed into my deep-rooted feelings of not being worthy or good enough, fuelling a foul belief system. Being on the path to 'healing' felt like an unachievable goal, in the far distant future and frankly not very kind. This felt contradictory to the practice of mettā, the practice I felt aligned with.

One day, with a heavy heart, I was out walking through a pine forest. With each step, I felt an increase of energy rise in my body and erupted through my lungs as my inner voice screamed, *I am not broken! Stop telling me that I'm broken and that I am not whole!* After a cathartic eruption of anger, frustration, despair and longing, I fell to the ground and sobbed. I stared into the forest and pleaded it to show me a more loving way to look at my life. I wiped away my tears and slowed my breathing, to listen. I felt the energy of the trees, birds, sunlight, dirt and wind rally together to hold me. The power of nature's embrace made me feel heard and supported. I contemplated about how nature is unapologetic and trusting, it surrenders to all conditions, it grows gently through its cycles and all beings work together symbiotically. I felt not only part of nature, but that I *am* nature. The sunlight dried my wet cheeks and invited me to be unapologetic as I moved through my life and that I needed to lean into trust more often. I asked the brisk wind and the pine trees, 'How can I be kinder to myself as I move through life?' Within mere moments, an orange and brown butterfly fluttered past me. I felt a wave of peace and relief wash over as my body remembered that much like a butterfly, it was also in a state of metamorphosis.

✦ **metamorphosis** *(noun)*

Greek for *transformation* or *change in shape*

Pain as a Portal

I continued to contemplate the word healing and how its definition implies that an element of brokenness is present. To be broken suggests a separation has taken place. To think or believe humans are broken is a construct of the mind only. In every moment, every experience, we are whole. That wholeness changes form, but never separates. That fact felt like the essence of mettā. Ever since that day, instead of using the term healing, I use the term *mettā*morphosis which I deem to hold the meaning:

> ✦ *mettāmorphosis (verb)*
> *having unconditional love and loving-kindness whilst transforming*

This acknowledges that humans are more complex than butterflies and our ability to trust and surrender to morph does not come easily to us, for many reasons. When humans feel vulnerable, which is often paired with pain, they sometimes need more guidance and loving-kindness (mettā) to trust and move through their phases.

When correlating my observations of the phases that I have gone through with my experiences, it came with much delight to see how similarly it could be compared to the 4-phase cycle of a butterfly. With this, a gentle philosophy to live by and an intentional process to move through our phases, was brought into form.

❖

PHASES OF A BUTTERFLY AND ANALOGICAL COMPARISONS

In the following pages, we will look at the phases of metamorphosis for a butterfly and translate this into an analogy for an indication of how we, as humans, can follow a similar sequence of *mettā*morphosis. One of the things I love about analogies, is the freedom of interpretation. This is only my interpretation, which I use as it feels gentle, yet true, based on my experiences and studies of human behaviour.

Below is a brief overview:

Metamorphic Phase of Butterfly	Analogical Comparison and Mettāmorphic Phase of Human
Phase 1 Egg	The creation of an experience
Phase 2 Caterpillar and feeding stage	The mind and body absorbs as much of the information about the experience as possible and responds to these stimuli with emotions
Phase 3 Chrysalis and physical morphing into butterfly	When a human is initiated into undertaking a period of change
Phase 4 Butterfly emerges from chrysalis	The human emerges with a sense of freedom from their pain along with a treasured gift or many

Pain as a Portal

PHASE 1

Metamorphic Phase of a Butterfly

Eggs are laid on plants by female butterflies. These plants will then become food for the hatching caterpillars. Females lay a lot of eggs at once so that at least some of them survive.

> **Analogical Comparison and Mettāmorphic Phase of a Human**
>
> Humans are birthed by their mother. Experiences are then continuously birthed by life. Imagine that every experience is an egg. The immediate surroundings will become food for the experience. This food could be people's reactions, words or actions that we witness and absorb to create thoughts, decisions, morals, memories etc. Life provides a lot of experiences to assist with survival.

PHASE 2

Metamorphic Phase of a Butterfly

There are usually five stages, or instars, between hatching and pupating, where the larva grows legs and becomes a caterpillar. As the caterpillar grows, each instar ends with a moult, where the caterpillar sheds its skin (which is eaten) and grows a new, larger one. During this phase, it eats as much as it can. The energy from the food eaten at this time is stored and used in phase three and four.

When caterpillars sense danger, such as a predator, loud noise, vibrations in their surroundings, or being touched, they respond with a range of defence mechanisms. Many have poisonous venom which is released through the tips of fine hairs or spines on their bodies when touched, while others thrash and bite their attackers, some writhe their bodies and shake their head repeatedly, some freeze, and some release a squeak or scream.

Analogical Comparison and Mettāmorphic Phase of a Human

After an experience has occurred, the body and mind absorbs as much information that can be gathered from that experience as possible, just like food. The mind forms decisions about whether the experience was pleasant, unpleasant, or traumatic, based on what emotion the body senses. This information is stored in the mind and body, to be used in phase three and four. This is where belief systems and cellular memories are formed. If the body feels threatened, it may respond with defence mechanisms such as crying, screaming, attacking, ignoring, denying, freezing, overthinking or over-consuming food, drugs, sugar and social media, to name a few.

PHASE 3

Metamorphic Phase of a Butterfly

When the caterpillar is fully grown and stops eating, it finds a place to moult and become a pupa, otherwise known as a chrysalis.

Depending on the species, the chrysalis may suspend under a branch, hidden in leaves or buried underground.

It may look like nothing is going on, but there are big changes happening inside. The caterpillar dissolves into a soup-like substance. Special cells that were present in the larva are now growing and transforming rapidly and will become legs, wings, eyes and finally, a butterfly. This process is called metamorphosis.

Metamorphosis is controlled by gene regulation. The changes that occur within each of the immature stages: egg, caterpillar and chrysalis, are controlled by various groups of genes which are turned on during the different stages of development. Therefore, the genes of the organism remain the same throughout the lifecycle, but different groups of genes are turned on and off throughout development. Many chrysalises interact with their environment by producing creaking, chirping or clicking sounds. It is theorized that the sounds are in response to external agitation and may be a defence mechanism or perhaps a way to inform potential mates in the area that they are getting ready to emerge.

The chrysalis gradually darkens in colour and becomes transparent as it nears the end of the metamorphosis, so that the wing colour and pattern is visible. As the muscles of the thorax expand, it splits the exoskeleton of the chrysalis near the apex. The butterfly's head emerges first, followed by the legs which are used to secure it to a perch. Next, the abdomen comes forth and rhythmically contracts up and down, pumping hemolymph (blood-like fluid) into the wing veins. The soft wings gradually expand with each contraction until they harden and are fully erect. The butterfly proceeds to excrete meconium, a liquid waste, and cleans its antennae by pulling them through a space on the forelegs. It fastens its two halves of the proboscis together, to produce a functional feeding tool.

Analogical Comparison and Mettāmorphic Phase of a Human

When a human's mind, body and spirit determines that they are ready to move onto the next phase, they enter a metaphoric chrysalis. Sometimes a person may feel very discontent with their situation or feelings and make an intentional decision to try and change. Sometimes a person may have resistance, and often an underlying fear of the unknown of what happens next. In these instances, it is common for people to metaphorically go 'underground' or get stuck in a state of deep rest, which is sometimes called depression or a dark night of the soul. The cells within the human body are rearranging and responsive to either option.

Despite being in this process, humans continue to interact with their environment. A person's defence mechanisms will be activated if they either are or perceive that they are under threat. These mechanisms are our fight, flight, freeze or fawn responses.

While in a metaphoric chrysalis, humans are undertaking massive changes, which are unseen to the external world. These changes can be physical, emotional, psychological or spiritual.

As a human starts to emerge, they will experience some clarity about themselves, and a breath of fresh air is often taken and a feeling of freedom from their pain begins. They often feel different, because they are. They get into the rhythm of their transformed self, often feeling a sense of release and expansion.

Pain as a Portal

PHASE 4

Metamorphic Phase of a Butterfly

Butterflies leave behind their chrysalis and take to the air on their new wings. Once they reach this stage of life, butterflies spend most of their time looking for a mate. Once the male inseminates the female, it soon dies. The female travels to find its host plant to lay its eggs on. Many butterfly species live for less than two weeks, while a few can live up to several months.

> **Analogical Comparison and Mettāmorphic Phase of a Human**
>
> When a human realises that they are out of their metaphoric chrysalis, they can often feel like stretching their metaphoric wings and see the world from a new perspective. They take to the air with a newfound sense of freedom from their pain.
>
> Once humans reach this stage, they often share their experience with a mate or the world. This heightened state of pleasure of freedom *feels* alive for less than a month, before the mind is consumed by a new experience, but sometimes this lasts much longer. The gift of this experience is however integrated into a human's cellular memory and psyche.

❋

THE CYCLE

I like to consider that from a macro-experience perspective, humans are in the complete state of mettāmorphosis, from birth to death. Within our lifetime, every moment and experience that occurs is a micro-experience of mettāmorphosis.

Therefore, we are typically in various phases of mettāmorphosis in response to multiple experiences, simultaneously. Experiences from childhood, past relationships, last year and from one-hour ago are all transforming within us. I imagine that our bodies or lives are like a butterfly house, with millions of experiences living inside of us, all at their natural phases, providing us the opportunity of 'life experience'.

It is no wonder that it can be hard to decipher what to do and where to go, with so much going on in the mind and body. From observing my own experiences, I have learned to trust the pain that is present and calling my attention, is the pain that is ready to be tended to.

I have developed The PAIN Process to assist you with navigating your way through all of your phases.

IMPLEMENTING THE PAIN PROCESS

The PAIN Process was developed as a tool, to serve as a lighthouse, guiding the way home, while still giving you freedom to experience all that is required, including going off path. The phases of mettāmorphosis are not to be mistaken for a ladder. They are phases within a natural cycle and no phase is better or worse than another. You cannot have one without the others.

The beauty of this process is that it will naturally happen whether you are aware of it or not. However, by intentionally engaging in this process, you will move through each phase in a way that empowers you to feel part of the process, rather than being the victim of it.

In my personal experience, since using The PAIN Process consciously, when I enter phase one, I have a sparkle of optimism about the upcoming journey. I move through each phase much quicker and with much less resistance to the process.

Using PAIN as an acronym, let's look closely at each phase and which intentional actions will assist you to move through each phase with loving-kindness. These intentional actions can be applied from this moment onwards because if an emotion is felt, it is telling you it's ready to be acknowledged.

As this process is based on an analogy, there are no strict rules or definite edges. Each phase serves only as a guide.

Pain as a Portal

THE PAIN PROCESS

	Phase	Metamorphic Phase of Butterfly	Mettāmorphic Phase of Human	Action
P	Phase 1	Egg	**P**ainful or **P**leasurable experience occurs	**P**resence
A	Phase 2	Caterpillar and feeding stage	**A**bsorption of information about the experience is undertaken by the mind and body and it responds with emotion	**A**cknowledge emotions with loving-kindness
I	Phase 3	Chrysalis and physical morphing into butterfly	**I**nitiation of undertaking change	**I**.C.E (Intentional Creative Expression) is applied with loving-kindness
N	Phase 4	Butterfly emerges from chrysalis	**N**ewfound gift/s emerge & a sense of freedom from the pain	**N**ourish your gift/s with gratitude, integration & sharing

PHASE 1

P = a **P**ainful or **P**leasant emotion arises in response to an experience

> ✦ **experience:** *(noun)*
>
> *an event or occurrence which leaves an impression on someone*

Action – **P**resence

An experience is in motion. There is nothing to actively do here as the body is amidst the experience, in real time, instinctually doing all it needs to do.

Some people find it cathartic to name the experience or to tell the story about where they believe the pain was born. If it comes freely, allow it. If recalling the initial experience brings a pain that feels unbearable, leave it be.

If you are working with this model for long-term pains, you may have such a large tapestry of painful experiences that the birthplace for the felt pain is not known, or in some cases, not remembered. I have found that naming or knowing the initial experience is not necessary or a prerequisite to enter the following phases. The body knows the root experience on a cellular level—in its cells—and the medicine is held within the following phases. For example, this is often the case with intergenerational pains where

Pain as a Portal

we were not present, but the pain has been passed down through our DNA from our parents or grandparents, either by conditioned belief systems or when the body has experienced forms of abuse.

―――― *Compassionate considerations for this phase* ――――

♥ If an experience is perceived as pleasant, a person is more likely to respond by being present, intrigued and sometimes they want to stay in the experience for as long as possible.

♥ If an experience is perceived as unpleasant or harmful, a person is likely to immediately respond with a stress response, which is to fight, flee or freeze. These are important responses to have, as they can help to keep us somewhat safe.

♥ Self-judgement of how we responded in the moment, is common in this phase. This is the first opportunity where you can hold some mettā for yourself, in your heart. You are learning. You did the best you could, with what you knew at the time.

―――――――――――― ♥ ――――――――――――

PHASE 2

A = **A**bsorption of information about the experience is undertaken by the mind and body and it responds with emotion

If an emotion creates a sense of pain, humans instinctively want to rid of the pain or avoid it by denial or repression. I have found that when you have the intention of ridding yourself *from* your pain, or you *ignore or deny* the pain, you send the message to the pain that it is wrong and is not welcome. This prolongs the experience of the pain and creates more suffering. It also tells the body that its messages are being ignored. They then may become louder.

Avoiding and denying parts of us perpetuates self-rejection. Every human wants to belong at some point in their life. If we yearn to belong in a group, and we do not accept ourselves *as we are*, it is unlikely that we will feel accepted by the group. Self-acceptance can be attained by acknowledging and welcoming all parts of us. As our psyche believes experiences and the emotional responses to the experiences are now parts of us, this means accepting those parts too.

There is something uncomfortable that resides in pain, that humans typically try to avoid at all costs. Sometimes it is purely the pain itself. Sometimes it is the shadow, the dark, the void, the abyss, the unknown. It can feel scary! Once we feel the sensation of being scared or anxious, the brain sends a message to the body to go into a stress response to *fight* the pain, take *flight* from the pain or *freeze* in the pain.

By saying *hello* to the painful emotion, we shift our initial measurement of the amount of pain. Through a lot of experimentation, with myself and others, I have found that by doing this from a loving sentiment, aka mettā, the feelings immediately feel *less* painful.

Let's look at this from another angle. Imagine going to a party and everyone ignored you.

Would you:

a) act out of character to try to fit in or to be noticed?

b) physically shrink or hide somewhere?

c) go home to escape?

d) yell at the people ignoring you, calling them names?

Our emotions do similar things in our body if we do not acknowledge them.

They may:

a) feel they are growing more uncomfortable, attempting to get our attention

b) change form and present themselves in the body as illness or ailment

c) temporarily seem buried, but then rise repeatedly and seemingly unprovoked

d) put on a disguise as a thought pattern like, I am un-lovable.

When we practice acknowledging all parts of ourselves, we are more able to feel a sense of belonging in the most important place on earth, our body and mind. I believe that our feelings are friends.

Action – <u>A</u>cknowledge emotions

> ✦ **acknowledge:** *(verb)*
> *accept or admit the existence or truth of. Recognize the importance or quality of*

Acknowledge your uncomfortable, painful or pleasurable emotions. Say hello!

How does this emotion feel in the body?
Heavy, light, spikey, dense, fluffy?
Name this sensation, _____.

Where do you feel this emotion in your body?
Head, heart, back, knee, chest, stomach, everywhere?
Name this place, _____.

Does this emotion have a colour?
Name it. _____.

Does this emotion have a feeling associated to it?
Sad, angry, lonely. Name them, _____, _____, _____.

When acknowledging your emotions, try to treat them like a new friend at your housewarming party. Be curious about them, kind, gentle and welcoming. This can be difficult, as resistance may rise, but it is important. Some examples could be having a conversation with them such as:

> *Welcome to my body, pain. You feel heavy and black. I feel sad and angry. I want to cry but I also want to scream. I also feel numb. I wonder how you will feel tomorrow.*
>
> *Hello despair. Welcome to this moment. You feel quite heavy in my chest and dark green. I look forward to seeing what you have to teach me.*
>
> *We meet again, joy. Welcome!*
>
> *Oh, hello contraction. You feel sharp and there is throbbing. I am listening.*

Alternative action

If you cannot label the emotion or not yet welcome it, or you do not subscribe to labels, simply acknowledge, *I am having an experience.*

Compassionate considerations for this phase

♥ It is natural in this phase for the mind to start thinking, even obsessing about the story of what you have experienced. Some people find a lot of benefit from storytelling as this assists to free themselves from the pain, others find that this is not beneficial for them as it keeps them feeling stuck in the pain of the experience, or victim of it. Try to notice how your body responds to the story.

♥ It is common in this phase for humans to contemplate whether what they experienced was fair or deserving. If you experienced any form of mistreatment, as part of practicing mettā, remind yourself that *no*, you were not deserving of being mistreated. Remind your mind, body and heart that the *pain* which has been the *response* to the experience is the portal in this model. You *deserve* only love, respect and kindness.

♥

Pain as a Portal

PHASE 3

I = Initiation of undertaking change

To assist us to remember this step, consider how when our body experiences physical pain, it is instinctual to *apply ice*, heat or pressure. When used appropriately, these actions reduce pain, the chance of sustaining a long-term injury and recovery time.

Action – **I**.C.E is applied

Engage in Intentional Creative Expression (I.C.E) or in short: Apply I.C.E with loving-kindness. Let's break this down into its three parts: Intentional (I), Creative (C) and Expression (E).

Intentional (I)

> ✦ *intentional (adj)*
> *done on purpose; deliberate*

Intention

I engage in this upcoming practice / activity to acknowledge, welcome, express and transform my pain into a gift. I will do so with utmost loving-kindness towards myself (mettā), to the best of my ability.

Making intentional choices or actions, increases the chances of attaining the desired outcome. For example, if your intention is to have a flourishing garden, you have the option to:

1. trust that flowers grow from seeds drifting in the wind, landing on soil, *or*
2. you can choose to actively plant seeds in the desired location.

With option two, there is statistically, a much higher chance of the seeds growing and flowering if you intentionally plant them.

To understand *why* we engage in Intentional Creative Expression, is another important step in being intentional. This is often called 'knowing your why'. This leads us back to emotion. The Latin derivative for the word emotion, is emotere.

> ✦ **emotere** (*noun*)
>
> *energy in motion*

The science of how emotions and feelings are formed is very complex and humans have only scraped the surface of what there is to know about how the brain and body works. Below is a very simplified explanation.

Step 1 – An experience occurs.

Step 2 – Energy within the body forms into a cell within the body. This combination of energy—neurons, neurotransmitters, peptides and hormones—creates a biochemical reaction, either contracting or expanding the cell, creating a physical sensation.

Step 3 – A signal is sent to the brain. If it signals a contraction of sensation, the brain labels this as a painful emotion. If it signals an expansive sensation, the brain labels this as a pleasurable emotion.

Step 4 – The brain then looks back at all the information available—past experiences, sensations, emotions, conditioning—and labels this emotion with a feeling, i.e. sad, happy, angry, scared.

Step 5 – We then respond, i.e. laugh, sweat, cry, freeze, fight, run.

As emotion is energy in motion, by design it is to be expressed and morphed. We can do this effectively by **Intentionally** and **Creatively Expressing** this emotion. If we do not express it, the energy becomes stagnant, stuck and contracted. This is how trauma, suffering and illness develops.

Creative (C)

> ✦ *creative (adj)*
>
> *relating to or involving the use of the imagination to create something*

We are all creative beings, simply by being alive. Breathing, thinking, speaking, moving and feeling all *creates* a unique frequency of energy. Sometimes, we allow our fear of making a mistake to stop us from being creative. Creativity is not a talent. It is an ability to play, experiment and surrender to the process.

Expression (E)

> ✦ *expression (noun)*
>
> *the action of making one's thoughts or feelings known*

Each pain is like a different breed of butterfly, requiring its own unique remedy and nourishment to morph. It is here that you must remind yourself that you are undertaking a mettāmorphosis: (*v*) *having unconditional love and loving-kindness whilst transforming.*

To have unconditional love and loving-kindness towards yourself and others is a lifelong practice. It requires patience and trust. Practicing this can be painful and poke a tender wound where we question whether we're deserving of unconditional love. While I can say with absolute certainty that **YES, YOU ARE**—you may not believe it until you have gone through the portal of this pain and come to that belief, realisation, resonance, remembrance or knowing yourself.

There is no rule of how many acts of Intentional Creative Expression (I.C.E) you must engage in to fully morph your pain. I encourage you to do what comes to your mind, body or heart. You may need to experiment with different forms of expression to find which feels like it is cathartic, a release, or enjoyable.

Your pain may require seven paintings, or twenty-seven. You may need to cry twenty-two litres of tears, or scream in a forest, write three poems, plant a vegetable garden or receive eighty-seven hugs. Your pain may require a year of daily meetings with silence, eleven sessions in therapy, tears shed in the shower often, weekly boxing sessions, three wood carvings, two weeks in a new country and a week spent in bed.

When we practice intentional creative expression regularly, we have clearer access to our essence, intuition, knowing or instinct. Butterflies and the entirety of nature live instinctively, and we can too, because we are nature. Humans are a complex species, which makes instinct harder to sense. The more you practice, the easier it will be to access. When you have a clear sense of self and purpose, you know you are whole.

―――― *Compassionate considerations for this stage* ――――

♥ While I could list a range of likely feelings and challenges you may experience during this phase, this does not aid your journey. External validation only serves the mind of humans, it does not assist you on a soul level. It is more helpful for you to know that no matter which feelings you experience, they are perfect for you and your unique time in this phase.

♥ Without actively and intentionally engaging in phases one and two, the more complex, confusing and painful this phase can be, as many experiences can feel like one big entangled unpleasant sensation.

♥ It is likely that feelings or emotions that differ from those acknowledged in phase two will rise while engaging in creative expression. Just as you have done in phase two, these sensations require your loving acknowledgement also.

♥ When a caterpillar enters its chrysalis, it is entering into something that assists to protect it and provides a space for it to transform. This suggests that we need protection too, as we enter our soup-like process. What are some boundaries or protective measures that you can put in place? Do you need more rest or downtime? Do you need a quiet space where you can be present and free from other responsibilities? Do you need support from a trusted allied health professional?

♥ Butterflies spend most of their life in phase three. They can spend anywhere from two months to two years in chrysalis. The time spent is dependent on their species but also in response to whether the external living conditions are optimal for growth. This is indicative of time spent in this phase for us too, is dependent on each individual, their previous experiences and whether their current living conditions are conducive to healthy growth. Looking beyond nature, scientific research agrees. If a person is not in an environment that is conducive for healthy growth, or they do not participate in intentional creative expression of their pain, it is easy to enter into a state of suffering or for the coping strategies to slowly or quickly develop into self-destructive responses, such as addictions. A self-destructive addiction is the fact or condition of being addicted to a particular substance or activity causing harm to a person's wellbeing. Some examples of this include overuse or underuse of drugs, exercise, working, eating, computer games, shopping, social media, limiting belief systems. I see these as *un*intentional expressions of pain.

Optimal external living conditions includes having access to our core human needs: nutritional food, water, shelter and being free from significant harm and abuse.

Optimal internal living conditions includes having self-compassion, love and gratitude as part of your daily mindset and nurturing belief systems that support living a healthy and fulfilling life.

♥ Attempting to rush to the next phase and/or being attached to the gift as a destination is likely to ignite more pain. Trusting the time spent in the metaphorical chrysalis is very difficult for humans. You are invited to practice patience, trust and non-attachment to the outcome of this phase. Thankfully, it is common to find, realise or experience some gifts whilst still in chrysalis. These gifts serve as food, sustenance and validation of natural growth to assist with the process.

―――――――――――――――― ♥ ――――――――――――――――

Glossary of I.C.E-cream toppings

Here you will find a glossary of some types of Intentional Creative Expression. These can be done alone or with a supportive, loving friend or professional. While I like to imagine that each pain is like its own species of butterfly, to add an element of playfulness, I also like to imagine that each pain is like its own ice-cream. The cone, cup or bowl is the experience, the different flavours of ice-cream are the different pains or pleasures, and the endless amounts of toppings are the many forms of Intentional Creative Expression that we apply to the pain.

I encourage your childlike self to allow your curiosity to try different toppings. You are allowed to have as many toppings as you need to make the ultimate recipe for your individual pain and circumstance. You may discover that you have your favourites, that you add to any or all of your pains or pleasures.

For example:

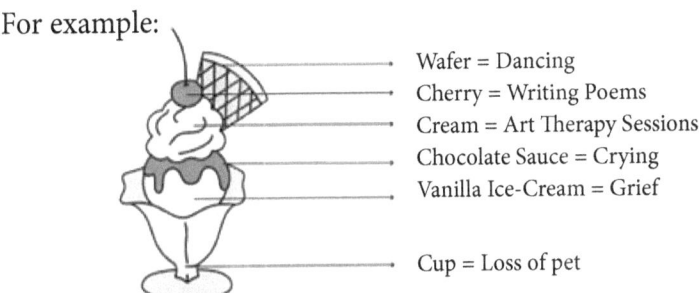

Wafer = Dancing
Cherry = Writing Poems
Cream = Art Therapy Sessions
Chocolate Sauce = Crying
Vanilla Ice-Cream = Grief

Cup = Loss of pet

Tip: There is sometimes a pressure or sensation in the area of the body that serves as a clue as to where or how the pain wants to be expressed.

For example, if there is pressure in your:

- throat: use your voice to talk, sing, yell, hum, chant
- hands: paint, punch a pillow, play in dirt, pat an animal
- chest: breathe
- full body: dance, hug, walk, lie in a bath

Intention

I engage in this upcoming practice / activity to acknowledge, welcome, express and transform this sensation / emotion / feeling of _____ into a gift.

Pain as a Portal

ALLOW the water to run over your body, washing the feeling away.

ASK the feeling how it wants to be expressed.

BELIEVE you are worthy of love and all of life's greatest gifts.

BLOW the feeling into a balloon and pop it.

BREATHE gently. On your inhale, welcome the feeling, on your exhale, let it go. Repeat until the feeling softens.

CLEAN whilst imagining the feeling slowly diminishing from your body.

COOK a meal that will nourish and care for the feeling.

CRY the feeling out.

DANCE the feelings by giving them movement and shape.

DRINK water to dilute and flush the feeling away.

FEEL the sun's rays permeate the feeling.

GAZE at the night sky and send the feeling up, up, up until it turns into star dust.

HUG the feelings, with loving hands or a blanket.

IMAGINE the feeling morphing into a gift of your choosing.

JUMP until the feeling feels released.

LAUGH the feeling into the atmosphere.

LEARN a new language, the language of your body, heart or intuition.

LISTEN to the whispered message from your body, heart, or spirit.

LOVE the feeling until it dissipates.

MAKE ART about the thoughts, feelings and gifts.

MAKE MUSIC with anything you have, pots, pans, pencils and instruments. Imagine the feeling travelling down your limbs, through the music maker, to create a sound.

MAKE the feeling a cup of tea. Sip it. Tell the feeling you're there for it.

MEDITATE in stillness to feel all there is to feel, including stillness and silence.

MOVE YOUR BODY in a way that releases endorphins, thoughts, and limiting beliefs.

PLAY, giggle, explore and experiment to transform the feeling with the magic of imagination.

RELEASE the feelings with acupuncture, massage, reiki or love.

SCREAM the feeling out.

SEND the feeling to the stratosphere with a gust of wind.

SHARE the feelings with a river.

SING about the thoughts, feelings, gifts.

SIT on the earth and send the feeling down into its core.

SMILE at the sensations.

SPEAK with an Allied Health Professional or trusted friend.

TAP the place where you feel pain, gently.

THROW the feeling away, like a ball.

WALK, run, skip, swim the feeling out.

WHISPER your thoughts about the feelings to an animal, flower or tree.

WHISTLE the song of the feelings.

WRITE a letter, poem or story about the feeling.

Pain as a Portal

Space to add your own:

Integration

> ✦ **integration** *(noun)*
>
> *the act or process of integrating*

Integration of your experience starts in phase two, acknowledging your sensations and feelings. It continues by engaging in Intentional Creative Expression. It is then fundamental to intentionally create some time and space for further integration after you have engaged in an activity of creative expression. It is beneficial to make time for this straight after the activity, however integration is also a process that occurs over time, both consciously and subconsciously. Intentionally creating some time to integrate honours the work you have done and the process you have engaged in. It also assists your body, mind and spirit to consolidate all the sensations, emotions, feelings, concepts, new information and learnings that it experienced while engaging in creative expression.

This assists the body to:

1. Make sense of, process or reflect on what it may have experienced during creative expression.
2. Remember the benefits of engaging in creative expression.
3. Decrease the chance of overstimulation or dysregulation of the nervous system by rushing to the next activity of daily life.

How long each person needs to integrate is different. It will take some experimentation for you to decide how long suits you best. You can spend ten-minutes, an hour, or more! How best to integrate

Pain as a Portal

is also different for everyone. Typically, the activity would be slow, calm and gentle, much like being in a chrysalis.

Some ways to integrate can include:

- Sitting with the sensations, feelings and learnings, and not doing anything with them.
- Sitting in silence, focusing on your breathing.
- Lying on the earth, in the sun, watching clouds pass by.
- Eating a nourishing meal.
- Sitting or walking in nature.
- Share with a friend or allied health professional, who's a respectful and active listener.
- Laying in a bath, river or ocean.
- Journalling.

PHASE 4

<u>N</u> = <u>N</u>ewfound gift occurs naturally

Much like a seed, the egg of a butterfly holds within its cells its fullest potential. Phase four, the butterfly, is the expression of this egg reaching its fullest potential. The butterfly itself is a gift to our earth. It plays an important role in the ecosystem. Butterflies are master pollinators. They help plants to produce fruits, vegetables and flowers by spreading pollen wherever they go. They also bring joy and inspiration to humans.

When the butterfly emerges from its chrysalis, humans witnessing this typically enter a state of awe. When I have witnessed people emerge from their metaphorical emotional chrysalis, I too enter a state of awe. The way they now hold themselves, the look in their eye and the energy they emit is breathtaking.

Humans do not know for certain how the butterfly feels once emerging, now with wings to fly, but what I have experienced and witnessed is that when humans emerge, they feel a *sense of freedom from their pain*. The pain is now dull, or a memory no longer ignites an intense physical sensation in the body. The pain no longer takes hold of them in their everyday life, their behaviours or in their dreams. With time, they become aware of the gift/s that have been hiding within the pain, waiting to be morphed. The gift is the pain reaching its fullest potential.

✦ **newfound** *(noun)*

something discovered, acquired or achieved

> ✦ **gift** *(noun)*
>
> *something given*

Each and every newfound gift is perfectly suited for you and your individual journey. Due to duality of all things, a gift to you, may be a pain for another. For example, rain for a farmer in drought may be a gift, however rain for a person who has experienced a life-threatening flood may be painful. The gift you discover is invaluable to you. It is physically, emotionally and spiritually yours, so it can never be taken from you. Sure, along the way you may forget where in the psyche you put it, but it is always kept there in safekeeping, for when the time is right to remember it. Our cells, subconscious and soul are magical like that. These gifts raise the vibration of your consciousness, which is a gift in itself. You may ask yourself how you'll know for sure that you've gotten to this phase. Trust *that you will know.* If, however, you have temporarily lost trust in knowing the signs of your body, I will share a few here and more in part three of this book.

These gifts may present themselves as:

- A realisation.
- A knowing.
- A feeling the body finds pleasure in experiencing.
- An energetic shift from within that you have no words for.
- A cellular remembrance.
- A sense of homecoming to oneself.

These gifts bring meaning and purpose to the pain. This is when you embody and feel in your bones, that pain can be a portal. Another way to know is to engage in some self-inquiry and reflect on what gifts came from this pain.

Some questions to contemplate are:

- Did my pain have a message for me?
- Did my pain want me to change something not in my best interest I'm doing?
- Did my pain lead me to something that has benefitted me?
- Did my pain bring me closer to better understanding myself, my values, what I stand for?
- Did my pain serve as a portal to joy, love, forgiveness or understanding?
- Would I be able to connect with others as deeply, if I don't connect with my pain?
- What have I learned about myself through this process?

Actions – <u>N</u>ourish your gift/s with integration, gratitude and sharing

1. Create some intentional time and space to integrate the feelings and learnings that have come with discovering your newfound gift.
2. Express gratitude for your newfound gifts. This can be done by feeling it in your body, dancing it, painting it or saying *thank you!* to life out loud. Gratitude beholds magic. It clears the storm clouds, showing that the sun was there all along. Gratitude is a way that we can share our gift with the universe, as an offering of feedback.

3. Some of your gifts may want you to take further empowered action. What that action looks like is different for everyone. It may be in the form of an apology, changing careers, moving towns, taking a break, ending a relationship, starting a relationship, cleaning out the shed, starting a new hobby, sharing your story with the world or something else that feels empowering and inspiring for yourself or others.

────── *Compassionate considerations for this stage* ──────

♥ Humans like to try to measure, score or judge experiences by size. If you find yourself questioning if your gift is big enough to prove that you have metaphorically entered phase four, the answer is yes. The part of us that asks this question is the part that wonders how the *world* will judge our gift or our process. This gift is for you, and only you. Its value will only be understood by you, as no-one else will understand specifically what it felt like to endure your journey. This is your opportunity to unapologetically rejoice in your gift as you deserve it for all you have endured.

PLEASURE AS A PORTAL

It is just as important for us to engage in The PAIN Process for our pleasant experiences. While experiencing pleasant feelings, the time spent from phase one to four can be perceived as quick in relation to a painful experience. Spending intentional time in each of the stages expands the potency of the experience further, so even more pleasure is experienced. This creates new neural pathways in the brain so it can recognise and welcome pleasure in the future. It also assists us to be less likely to fall into victimhood or hopelessness when we experience a painful experience, as the body and mind remembers that it has experienced plenty of pleasure.

―――――― *Compassionate considerations* ――――――

♥ Whilst engaging in The PAIN Process for pleasurable experiences, it is common to want to hold on to the pleasure. We tend to think it is rare, so we grasp onto it. When we try to hold on to something beyond its natural timeframe, often there can be an underlying fear of grief or loss which ignites a pain. To keep an experience pleasurable and to prevent it from morphing into pain, practicing trust and willingly letting go while it is still pleasurable, will keep it in its true form.

―――――― ♥ ――――――

THE DIFFERENCE BETWEEN SELF-SOOTHING, I.C.E AND SELF-CARE

The activities that can be implemented for self-soothing, Intentional Creative Expression and self-care can be the same. The difference between them is the intention.

Self-soothing is any behaviour or activity that an individual uses to comfort or *nurture* themselves to soothe their strong emotions.

Intentional Creative Expression is any activity that an individual engages in to welcome, acknowledge and morph their emotions into a gift.

Self-care is an activity that has been planned in advance, to look after an individual's health and well-being. These activities *re-source* us with energy or life-force.

It is very important to combine the use of self-soothing, I.C.E, self-care and integration activities regularly in your life. This combination provides you with the ultimate expression of loving-kindness and assists you to create the optimal internal living environment, within your mind, body and spirit.

✸

DIAMOND METTĀMORPHOSIS TEMPLATE

The image holds the many facets of Mettāmorphosis, to serve as a visual reminder that we are held and supported by many forces during our many phases. The diamond symbolises love, patience and strength. Diamonds are formed when carbon atoms bond together under intense heat and pressure deep within the earth. Like a diamond, we have a natural ability to adapt, develop and reach our potential from pressure or pain. We are held in time and space by the directions of North, East, South and West. Each point of the diamond holds each phase that we reach or cycle through. The points offer a pathway of how to get to the next point or phase, with loving-kindness. Within the diamond are other practices to adopt, to support your journey, no matter which phase you are in.

Phase 1 is held externally by the alchemical symbol of the element of Earth, to represent our current experience of life on Earth, birth and death. Phase 2 is held externally by the alchemical symbol of the element of Water, representing the emotions, cleansing and renewal. Phase 3 is held externally by the alchemical symbol of the element of Fire, representing transmutation, generation of energy and wisdom. Phase 4 is held externally by the alchemical symbol of the element of Air, representing freedom and connection to your spirit. At the centre holds the element of Aether, representing our spirit or soul, where all aspects of ourselves reside.

Each of these phases, practices and supports, hold the balanced energy of yin (black, dark, feminine) and yang (white, light, masculine), to assist you with realising your wholeness, balance, unity and harmony within.

Diamond Mettāmorphosis template

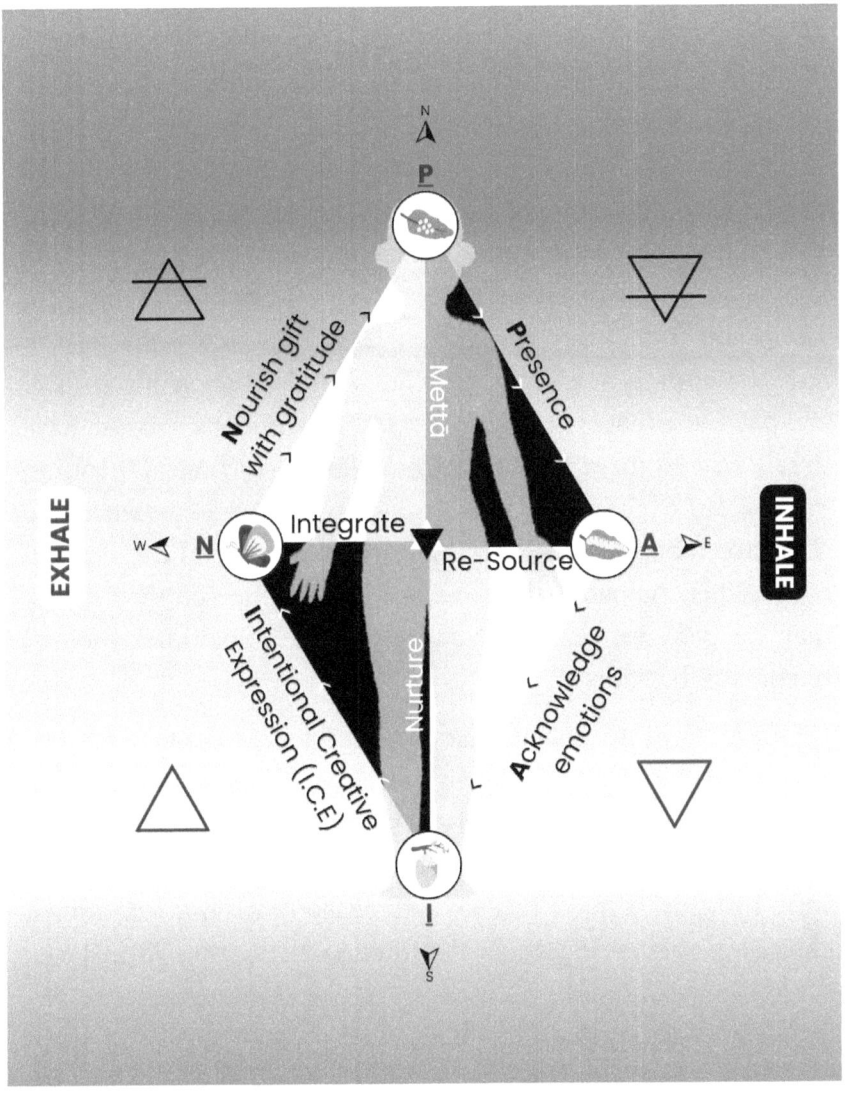

FUTURE PORTALS

While morphing *pain* has been the focus of this book, by engaging in The PAIN Process you will also learn many skills that will assist you to play your part in creating the future that you desire. Experiences don't always happen *to* us. We make hundreds of choices every day that impact our experiences. For example, you invite your favourite friend to join you for a walk in a rainforest, you attend an art class, you drink that extra glass of wine, you go to a dinner party hosted by someone you don't get along with or you pat a dog that is growling at you. The emotions you will have in response to these experiences are often predictable. Of course, unexpected experiences may arise alongside the experience you chose to embark on. The goal is to make intentional choices that have a likely outcome of you experiencing what you desire. This may be play, joy, laughter, curiosity, determination, peace or freedom to be yourself.

I have come to believe that *all* experiences happen *for* me. Sometimes I sit back and go completely with the flow with what the Universe delivers me. While gifts are always provided, I can often feel confused, lost and a victim of my circumstances when I live like this. When I take an active step in making intentional choices, so that *my life* is an act of Intentional Creative Expression, life feels much more sacred, meaningful, synchronistic, supportive, expansive, exciting and incredible.

I invite you to play with being intentional, if you aren't already, into your choices, activities, words you use and way that you move through life. While life may offer us abundant access to pain, it also offers us abundant access to its many *gifts*.

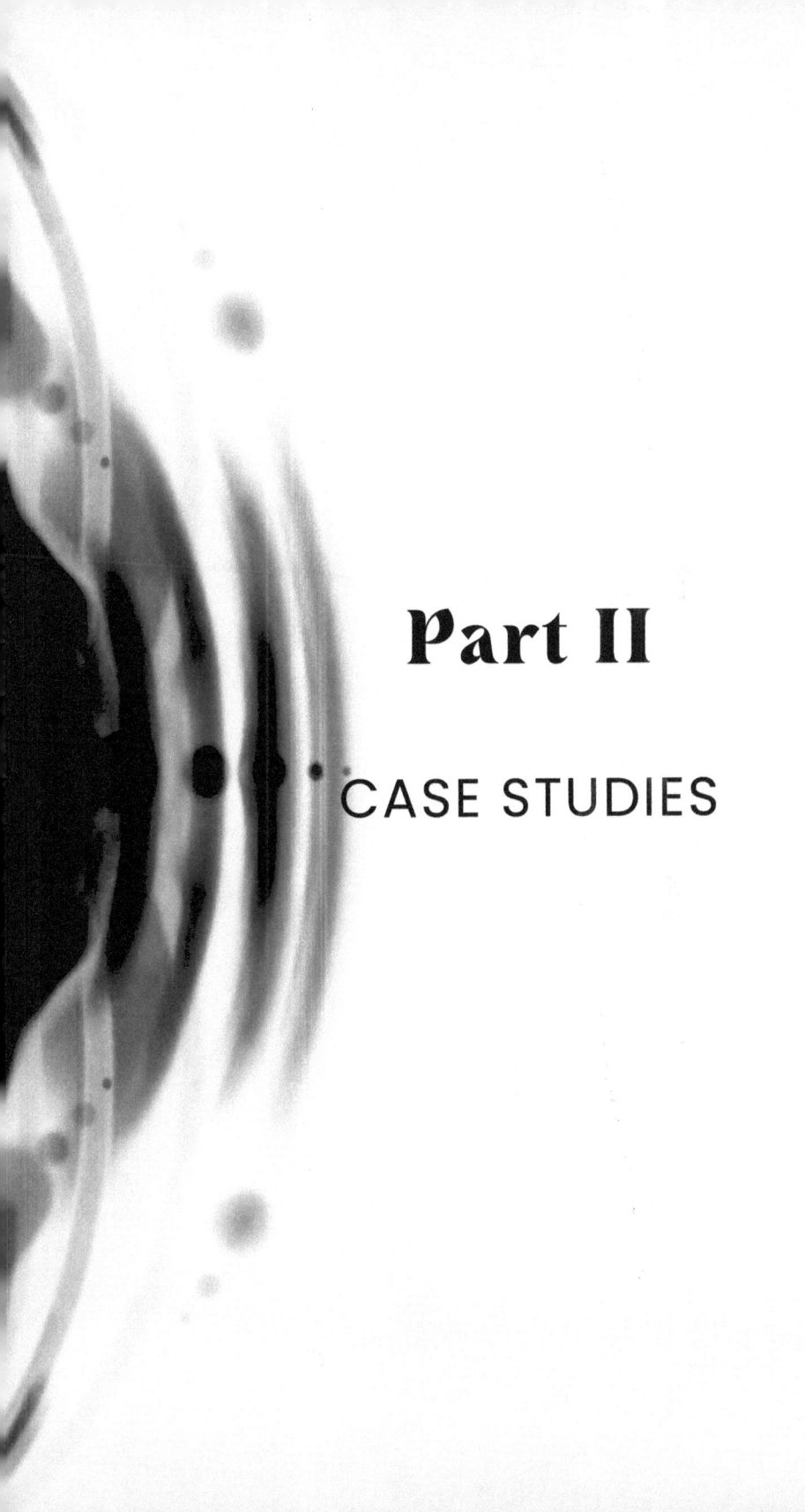

Part II

CASE STUDIES

This section offers five case studies based on my own experiences. The intention of sharing these, is to show a brief and practical example of what you have learnt in Part One and an introduction on how I incorporate The PAIN Process into my life.

Case Study 1
EXAMPLE OF PHYSICAL PAIN

PHASE 1

Painful experience that occurred: Menstruation

PHASE 2

Acknowledge emotion: I felt nauseous, tired, irritable and a little bit sad. The pain in my womb space fluctuated between a stabbing sharp pain and a dull pain.

PHASE 3

I.C.E is applied:
- I breathed slowly. I imagined every breath in was breathing into the centre of the pain near my left ovary. On every breath out, I imagined breathing the pain out into the atmosphere. This was repeated for ten minutes until the pain subsided considerably.
- I repeated the above a few more times during the day when intense pain would re-visit.
- I asked for hugs from my boyfriend while releasing big sighs.

Case Studies

The dull pain throughout the day was nurtured and integrated by laying in a hot bath, listening to gentle music, and occasionally rubbing the area, telling it that it's loved.

Time spent in this phase: 1 day

PHASE 4

Newfound gift/s occurs: A beautiful *reminder* that this time every month slows me down and that moving gently and gracefully creates more space for *peace.*

Case Study 2
EXAMPLE OF EMOTIONAL PAIN

PHASE 1

Painful experience that occurred: My Sandplay Therapy Trainer passed away.

PHASE 2

Acknowledge emotion: I felt grief flood by body and mind. I felt so sad that I lost my breath. My heart felt like it was aching. My mind couldn't think properly. This was my initiation into grief. I felt alone, lost and abandoned in my craft. I also felt relief, as she was in an immense amount of pain leading up to her death.

PHASE 3

I.C.E is applied:
- I cried. A lot.
- I told stories about how I thought she was a phenomenal human, how her smile lit up any room. I spoke of how she had taught me my art – the way to best dive into the heart of a pain and how to hold space for others to self-resolve theirs.

- I took time off work to do my best to honour this pain, her life and integrate.
- I wrote her letters – thanking her for sharing her wisdom, care, kindness and honesty.
- I lit candles and stared at her photo, sobbing some more.

<u>Time spent in this phase: 3+ months</u>

PHASE 4

Newfound gift/s occurs: Suddenly, I felt her presence instead of the pain. Simply by closing my eyes, I could see her smile, hear her laugh, and feel her joy. Memories of her comforting words and philosophies of life felt like whispers. The ache of missing her visits, but only for a few moments before I feel her essence hug me.

Case Study 3
EXAMPLE OF PSYCHOLOGICAL PAIN

PHASE 1

Painful experience that occurred: Having the thought, *What is the purpose of being a human?*

PHASE 2

Acknowledge emotion: I feel lost, confused, fearful, scared and dumfounded.

PHASE 3

I.C.E is applied:
- I meditate, dance, make art.
- I explore and process the concept of life and its associated pains with my therapist.
- I ask lots of questions to humans I meet, to get their point of view.
- I read lots of texts about mysticism, spirituality, science, poetry, near-death experiences, existentialism, philosophy.
- I cry.

Case Studies

- I travel.
- I spend time in nature and try to listen to any wisdom it wants to share.
- I try lots of new experiences.
- To integrate, I like to lie in the sun, journal, have a bath, take deep breaths and process with my therapist.

Time spent in this phase: 30+ years

PHASE 4

Newfound gift/s occurs: I have not yet fully emerged from this pain. I do, however, feel relatively close to emerging. I receive daily gifts of realisations where I am filled with love, joy and excitement and a big internal, *Yes! THIS is the purpose of living!*

Alas, this question holds a deep pain deep inside of me. It often rises to the surface when I experience an acute pain that takes a long time to diminish, and I doubt all that I think I know.

Case Study 4
EXAMPLE OF EMOTIONAL PAIN

PHASE 1

Painful experience that occurred: I am unsure specifically. Most likely a combination of many pains, ignored or stacked atop of each other in order to carry on.

PHASE 2

Acknowledge emotion: I felt completely exhausted. I felt void of most feelings.

PHASE 3

I.C.E is applied:
- I slept significantly more hours than usually required.
- I cried and cried some more.
- I bathed every evening in hot water while listening to music with no words or watched a TV series that didn't require much of my attention.
- I quit one of my jobs.
- I explored this experience with my art therapist.

- I swung on my outdoor swing, gently breathing.
- I limited my phone use and consumption of social media.
- I said no to any activity that ignited stress or unpleasurable feelings within me.
- I took a break from work.
- I patted my dog.
- To integrate, I spent significant amounts of time lying down either with eyelids closed or watching clouds, feeling all of the sensations and thoughts dance around in my body.

<u>Time spent in this phase: 4 weeks</u>

PHASE 4

Newfound gift/s occurs: I could feel my *nervous system regulate*, thoughts *calmed* and *grace* to move through life returned. I was *rejuvenated with energy, determination and clarity* on my capacity, how I want to use my energy and how I can create more space for rest and calm in my day to day.

Pain as a Portal

Case Study 5
EXAMPLE OF EMOTIONAL PLEASURE

PHASE 1

Pleasurable experience that occurred: Lying in bed, in the nook of my boyfriend's armpit, with my dog in arm's reach.

PHASE 2

Acknowledge emotion: I feel safe, peace, joy, love, serenity, and connection.

PHASE 3

I.C.E is applied:
- I smiled.
- I nuzzled in and told my boyfriend that I love him. I stroked his soft skin with this love. I planted smooches on his cheek.
- I patted my dog's silky, soft fur and told him I love him.
- To integrate, I closed my eyes to absorb all the pleasurable feelings that were swirling around my body.

Time spent in this phase: 15-30 minutes

PHASE 4

Newfound gift/s occurs: I was flooded with *gratitude* and *calmness*. I wondered how I ever got so lucky. I got very sleepy and had the most *peaceful sleep*.

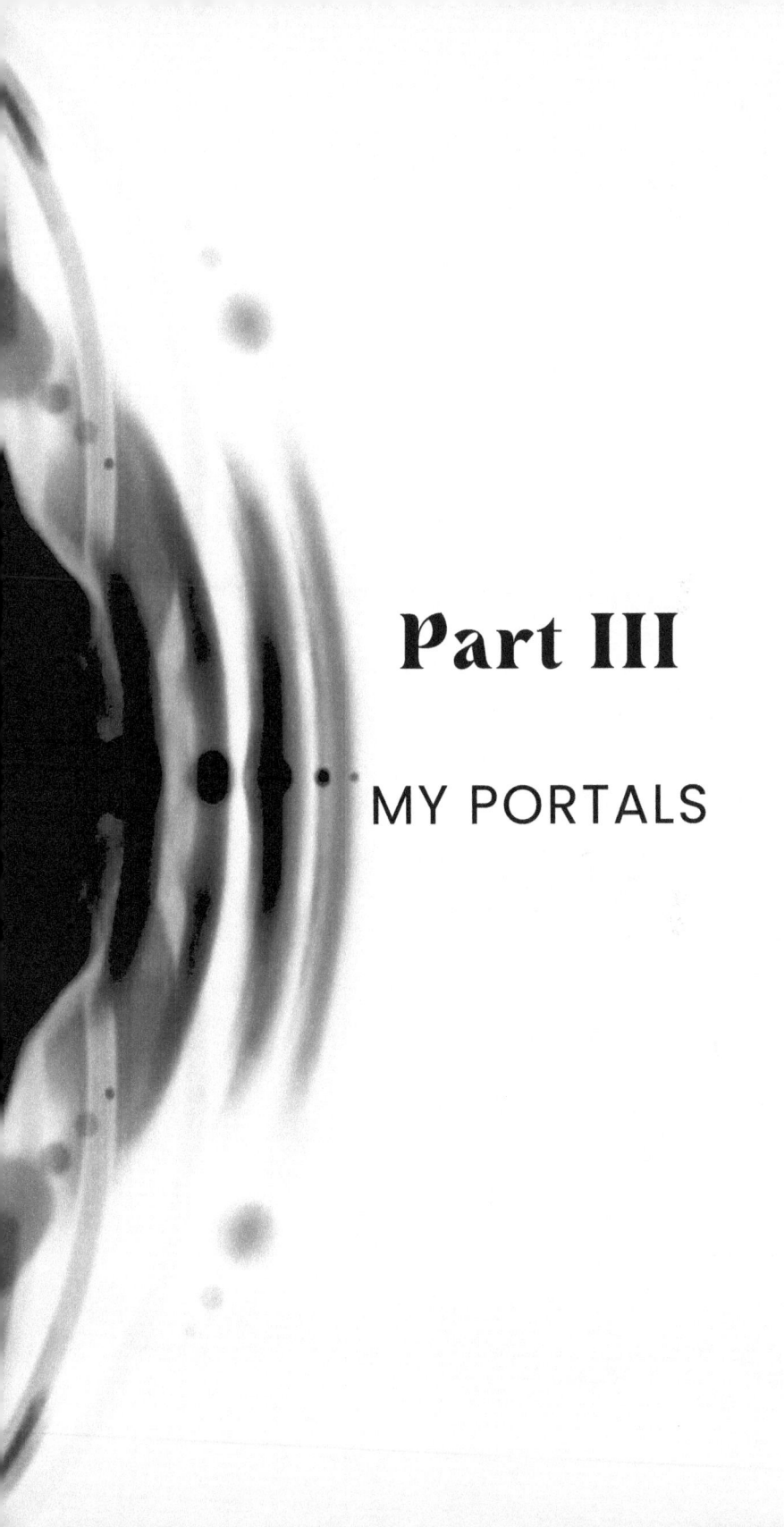

Part III

MY PORTALS

Let's explore some of my portals. As I started to write this book, these were the experiences, feelings and contemplations that felt like they were asking to be shared. This part is therefore written in a narrative format. My intention behind sharing these is to provide the story of how this practice came into my life, and how it has worked wonders in my life. As I began writing, it became clear that writing and sharing these stories was also an act of Intentional Creative Expression that my pains needed. So, these stories are for you, and for me.

I want to acknowledge that reading my story may distract you from your own. I encourage you to hold an intention for what you would like to get out of reading part three. This intentionally leaves space for you to fall in love with *your* story and storyline. Because that is where you will discover your most valuable gifts.

♥

I spent the first twenty-five years of my life living unintentionally, these periods of time were messy. I very much lived in the story of my experiences and did not express my pains. I suppressed, ignored and denied all of them, and this was when I suffered most. When writing them down, I found them difficult to simplify and separate. So, I have somewhat condensed them, while also leaving them as they are—messy and intertwined. This is much like a

Pain as a Portal

wound itself, twisted together by many components. The exact order of events is not of high importance to encapsulate the gist. There are experiences within experiences. Portals within portals within portals.

The various phases reflect how I currently feel about them, frozen in time, whilst writing this transmission. By the time you are reading this, they may have already morphed into something else. Emotions are just moving energy, always in motion, after all. How bizarre and delightful.

Acknowledging my emotional responses and then implementing Intentional Creative Expression has made my experiences feel clear and meaningful. I will share approximately how long I felt like I was in a chrysalis state for each experience. You will notice that when I wasn't intentionally using The PAIN Process, the time spent in chrysalis was significantly longer. This has served as validation of the beauty and power of applying I.C.E to the pain. The forms of creative expression I used along the way were many, so only some have been mentioned for a snapshot of my process.

As I began writing, each chapter ignited an immense feeling of vulnerability and energetic charge. While there was a sense of relief to honour my stories and to finally close them, writing them down didn't express enough of the energy alive in my body. So, I *painted* the pain and the gift. The sensations were friends within me, and I decided to honour them by giving them life outside of my body. The combination of words, colours and shapes felt like a truer expression of my truth as I felt it. As I surrendered to this process, it felt like each word and colour created an emotion and memory which created another word followed by another colour—creating another emotion, a memory—and so forth. This process took me on a wild emotional and mystical ride. At times it was exhausting. At times it was exhilarating. I took notes along the way, which are shared at the end of each chapter.

Each painting was created on wood, to assist in grounding me. The centre was carved out of each piece of wood to symbolise how the no-thing-ness of life has served me as portal and an opening to the many gifts' life has to offer. To be able to see through to the other side is a glimpse of our potential, but we don't know until we go there, and it takes intentional action, courage and trust.

Each piece was first painted black, to symbolise where it all began, within the darkness of the womb, life's most spectacular chrysalis.

Each piece of wood has a painting of the pain on one side and a painting of the gift on the other side, this symbolises wholeness. The pain is not separate to the gift. They are one. They are within each other—a team.

Each artwork is hooked together to symbolise that all of my experiences contribute to my wholeness. A single strand of beads has been intertwined in and around each artwork to symbolise the daily gifts that have been an ever-present adornment to my life. Each bead symbolises every day I have been alive to date—every day a gift.

NOTE

Throughout Part Three, I use the following symbols, to symbolise:

- a break in time
- ☐ implementation of Intentional Creative Expression
- ✸ gifts along the way

❁

confusion as a portal to gratitude

PHASE 1
My birth.

PHASE 2
Ages 1-17

My childhood was the foundation for all that was to come. I don't have many memories of my childhood, but time has shown that I soaked in more information about the world than my memory recalls. When I close my eyes and think of my childhood, a sensation I feel most in my body is *confusion*, so much confusion.

    My parents, sister and extended family were a tapestry of confusing things to my young mind. Sometimes there was safety, love, play, laughter, learning, yummy food and fun. Other times

Pain as a Portal

there was the opposite, which I now know were my family members own challenges, which they expressed through depression, post-traumatic stress, suppressed emotions, abusive behaviours, addictions, neurodivergent features and limiting belief systems. Of course, as a child, I didn't know why, but I always knew that these expressions weren't them at their core. I don't know how, but my joy, love and curiosity didn't diminish completely. It ebbed and flowed naturally, but at my core was always an infinite amount of love for my people.

I wanted nothing more than for people to be happy and if they weren't, I would strive to try and make them happy and care for them. I loved to share my thoughts, experiences, opinions, art, stories, joy and wonder of the world. People's responses to this ranged from pure adoration, to indifference, to disgust, to rage. At a very young age, I realised that humans were very unpredictable and that being me in my essence was risky business, often unsafe, but mostly, heart-wrenchingly disappointing. I began to keep my joy and many parts of me to myself. I can recall one of my favourite places for a time was in my cupboard. Hiding in the dark, alone, as I pressed up against the soft clothes it felt safe and peaceful.

Childhood was where some of my most painful decisions and belief systems about myself were born. Some of these were that I wasn't good enough, that I wasn't loved, that something was wrong with me and that I deserved how I was treated. Psychology has taught me that these are core wound decisions. Those unconscious decisions played out in many ways which you, the reader, will come to learn through our time together.

Then, there was school and friendships, which provided me with another tapestry of all of the emotions imaginable, painful and pleasurable. A strong memory I hold was that if I was ever slightly less chirpy than usual, I would get overwhelmed with people asking, 'What is wrong,' always delivered with a sense of panic, rather than care. Sometimes, I was just tired. Other times, I felt a deep sadness. I'd avoid sharing the truth and how I was feeling as I rarely felt satisfied by most people's responses to my pain, so, I hid it.

Still, to this day people tell me that they remember me as being so-care-free-and-happy. They are astounded when I tell them that I was, but a lot of the time it was a mask.

The beauty of not holding many memories, is that most of the pain that would be reasonable to assume to be present, simply is not. For the memories that did carve their way into my body and psyche, they were suppressed and denied until they came to the surface in my mid 20s. These memories are all tied to physical, verbal, emotional abuse and feeling like I was not fit for this world, based on what I did yearn from the world.

PHASE 3
Approximately ages 17-21

The older I got, the more I attempted to alter myself, beyond what was necessary, in an attempt to fit in or to keep the peace. I continued to act happy and fine. I mastered the act. My chrysalis was apparent due to my numbness. Within the numbness was my low self-regard and an almost inability to say no. An example of my lack of no looked like, sleeping with men who showed interest. For some, the interest may have been mutual, but for most, something within feared what they would do if I said no to their sexual advances, so I would talk myself into the possibility of feeling some form of aliveness and connection. More often than not, this resulted in amplified feelings of loneliness, shame and disappointment. My lack of acting on my internal no resulted in being in many relationships and situations which resulted in mistreatment. The mistreatment was a smorgasbord of verbal, financial, physical, emotional, sexual and psychological abuse which each formed their own cycle of mettāmorphosis to endure. These adult experiences had much more of an impact on me than anything I endured during early childhood.

I worked forty to fifty hours a week and studied simultaneously. Back then, I thought it was simply so I could be making enough money to live, but time proved that was not true. I favoured this form of distraction over the emotional agony I was in (Hello, coping mechanism!), tied in with a genuinely strong love to interact and serve.

As much as I feel hurt, I love humans deeply. I love them at their core, despite their actions. So, with my bursting desire to understand people better, I studied part of a psychology degree. I was too eager to work with the people, so I moved on to study various community services instead. At age twenty, one of my greatest gifts was when my community services teacher acted on her intuition about what service I would enjoy working in. As part of the certification, volunteer work placement was required. I had requested to go to the local women's refuge as my first preference along with about four other services. When the class was all receiving their placement information, she handed me mine, quickly saying, 'Don't freak out, let's talk after class.' I had been assigned my last preference, at a local day program for people with disabilities. I was enraged. *Why would she do this?* She explained that she felt I would love this work, and if I tried it, then at least I would know for sure. I was so nervous and scared. I didn't know how to be around people with disabilities, let alone be responsible for their safety. Well, with some brilliant guidance from other staff members, within a few hours of being with them, I knew I was home. They were unapologetically themselves. Some were loud and quirky; some were quiet and couldn't speak. Each person was unique with what support they needed. Some were very challenging to care for, while others felt easy. I realised I had been using the skills necessary to work in this environment my whole life.

✸ I am so grateful for my teacher, for really seeing me, my strengths and unwavering love for humans of all kinds. This was where I could finally be more 'me' than I had felt able to in a long time. While my roles in which I have supported people with disabilities have regularly changed over the years, these experiences have taught me countless things about myself, life and humans.

•

✸ Calling my sister, going for cake, juice, chats and a game of scrabble was one of the gifts that served as sustenance along the way. Imagining and remembering these times, immediately brings me a sense of calm and a smile on my face.

•

I went on to simultaneously work at the local youth homelessness refuge and then as a support worker for a community justice program, supporting Aboriginal men with disabilities integrate back into community after spending time incarcerated. While I loved these roles, and the people I supported, it came with

Pain as a Portal

immense challenges. The roles reflected back to me a lot of what I had experienced in my childhood and really, I was basically still a child.

✸ I spoke with a friend about my inner pull to see the world and he immediately encouraged me to listen to this call before I got trapped in the world of social welfare. So, I decided to do a short tour around Europe with a dear friend followed by moving to England with a one-way ticket. At the time, I thought I was in a pretty good place with my mental wellness. Undertaking this journey soon started to uncover that I was in fact, not in a good place. As money quickly dissipated, I did short stints of babysitting, hospitality and cleaning, but all of these roles invoked a deep sense of boredom. Feelings of fear, panic and sadness started to flood my body.

✸ I went to a bookstore and a book with the title, *The Magic* by Rhonda Byrne, caught my attention. It consisted of twenty-eight days of daily exercises of gratitude. I started straight away. Every day little miracles happened. Amazement and curiosity started to grow within me again.

PHASE 4

I was fourteen days into the book when I felt a rush of energy throughout my body. My heart felt like it was bursting open. It felt like I was feeling gratitude for the first time *in* my life, *for* life—for *my* life. This was a love like no other, where my mind, body and soul symbiotically felt it much more intensely than ever before.

It suddenly dawned on me, like the sun reaching in and lighting up a cave for the very first time, that my heart was overflowing with *gratitude* for having had some gorgeous friends throughout my life. I had always known that I appreciated them, and would express this often, perhaps even over the top, but this sensation of gratitude for them woke me up from a spell. There were a select few that I felt completely seen by. And they loved me, regardless of the parts I deemed undesirable. They showed me in many ways. I was flooded with the memories of these ways. Their love and friendship fuelled me throughout my childhood and teenage years. What an abundance of gifts I had been given along the way.

I started to contemplate the major experiences that created the most pain, up until this point, all of which offered at least one thing to be grateful for.

It felt like my gratitude was eating away my confusion, fear and sadness. It was very difficult to feel scared with this much gratitude in my body. This was an absolute relief. Gratitude fuelled my being for a few weeks, leading me into my next chapter.

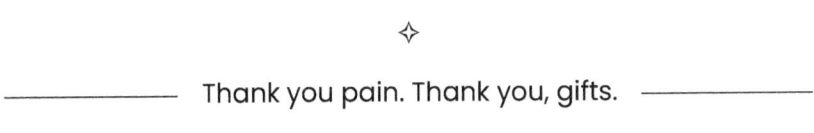

Thank you pain. Thank you, gifts.

Pain as a Portal

PORTAL PAINTINGS

☐ I started *'confusion'* by painting a portal portraying up to ten generations along my maternal and paternal lines. This very much felt like adult April expressing the clarity of intergenerational wounding. Child April then wanted to play. She painted her hands to do handprints and drew her house. I was amazed at how many memories started to flood in, of the pain and pleasure growing up. Friends that I hadn't thought of in years, my mum and dad's divorce, going between houses every second weekend, complaining to each parent about the other, getting a job at age eleven, being school captain at both primary and high school, my neighbour's cat having kittens, building cubby houses, my grandma and grandpa coming to visit on Wednesdays which also meant a Paddle Pop, laughing with my sister, being a nasty teenager to my family, loving sweets, the dolphin picture that hung above my bed, being very jealous of my sister as I thought she was the best thing, our pet Cockatiels and their funny habits, loathing my body, being a teacher's pet, preferring time with adults over teenagers, holidays, Rodney McDiscipline — the giant wooden spoon, Grandma's cooking, Grandpa's garden and photography, Pop's collection of clocks that had all stopped, Nan's big hugs and ice-cream, liking having only boy cousins, Mum helping me with school projects, horse-riding with Dad, loving going to friend's houses for sleepovers and much more. Where have these memories been living? It was very unexpected to have these, all while painting with my fingers.

As I added the glitter, I sobbed with so much gratitude for my childhood because it played such an important part in building who I have been and become. I went outside to check the mailbox while the tears ran. My neighbour came over to ask if I was okay because he hadn't seen me in a while. While sobbing I told him I was hibernating while I painted about some old pains. For a split second, I considered wiping my face and saying I was fine with a pretend grin, but I'm much better now at not acting on that thought, and instead showing up as I am. He responded with, 'I hope solitude and painting brings you what you need. Our pain most definitely needs to be nurtured sometimes. We love you, so if you need anything, let us know.' His message was a gift that ignited gratitude within me, a clear indication to start painting the other side of this portal.

Painting *'grateful'* was an extremely pleasurable experience. I smiled the entire time. I lovingly thought of my immediate family members now and see how much they've changed and grown for the better. I see the effort they have put in, to better respond to their pain. They didn't use the method in this book, however they did it in their own way. They are living tribute that we can come together at the same destination, via different paths.

'confusion'
as a portal to
'grateful'

hopeless as a portal to hopeful

In England, while beaming with gratitude, I decided to apply for a job as a live-in carer. I got the job and spent my twenty-first birthday in Dementia training. At the time, I was excited. Now, I see that as a glaring red flag, but hindsight is a bittersweet treasure. As I had previous experience as a carer, I was assigned various placements where the people required a broad range of care needs. Their file that I was shown before the placement was never an accurate representation of their needs, to say the least. I'd like to say if I saw the truth of their situation, I would've turned down many of the placements, but if I am honest with myself, 'no' was still a term rarely used. I also liked a challenge. What a sticky combination. What I experienced at these placements, with little to no support, led me down a path that got 'darker' every step of the way.

Pain as a Portal

PHASE 1

There was no single experience, it was months of experiences. At the time though, I was not aware of the build-up of repressed emotion, and I thought that the source of my pain was from being placed with a ninety-six-year-old lady, let's call her Aqua, who had advanced dementia. It was deemed unsafe for Aqua to leave her home because of her frailties, memory loss, verbally abusive tendencies and more. I was meant to get two hours off a day, but I came to an agreement with her daughter that I would bank these hours up in lieu of a full day on the weekend. Unfortunately, for multiple reasons, this didn't come to fruition and eventually meant I hadn't had a break or been outside other than to hang the washing, for over a month. Perhaps more. I lost count.

Aqua experienced high levels of anxiety and insisted on always being next to me, often holding hands. At bedtime, she continuously wailed, asking for her daughter and to go home, for hours, until she fell asleep. Music, books, television and having curtains open invoked severe paranoia for her, so they weren't an option for respite. Once a fortnight, Aqua would suddenly have an increase in energy and was able to walk independently and acted like she was thirty. On one of these occasions, Aqua experienced hallucinations and believed that I was her maid. She insisted that I cook food and offer it to all of her guests at the party she was hosting. When I initially declined, she threatened me with a knife. So, we had parties where she spoke and laughed with imagined people for hours, until she became exhausted. When her body caught up, she was so exhausted that she couldn't walk and would sleep for a few days. She would then come back to her baseline state.

PHASE 2

I contacted my employer multiple times asking for a break or to be taken out of this placement because I was feeling exhausted, isolated, alone, abandoned and not myself. They either didn't respond to my calls or emails or dismissed me by telling me I was doing great and that I was okay. I decided that my feelings must not matter and that I had to stick it out. I felt **hopeless**.

PHASE 3

Years and years ...

I felt a slow internal descent into a dark sense of reality. I felt like the darkness was claiming me and that I was slowly falling and losing myself. It was no doubt the void, within me. It felt like outer space, void of stars, yet with a strong and powerful energy.

For many months I considered whether dying was my only option to escape the pain of living. The voice usually said, *It would be easier if I just died*, or *What's the point?* and felt like a closed question, with no room for contemplation. I could feel my inner light and energy for life dim more and more every day. One day, I tried to feel or connect with the speckle of light that was left within my belly, yearning for it, and it wasn't there. When I say light, it is not a literal light that I can see inside me. This light symbolised a presence that felt like a spark of life force. It felt like complete darkness. I felt empty. I couldn't take the emotional turmoil any longer. With heavy breaths, I started planning my exit, to leave this body and earth far behind. I gathered Aqua's medication and

Pain as a Portal

sat it on the bench to consume. I wrote an urgent email that would be sent to Aqua's daughter and care company manager detailing that Aqua needed immediate care because I was leaving. Nothing else, no letters to family or friends, I hadn't even considered this. As I stared at the email and the medication, I closed my eyes one last time to get a glimpse or feeling of my light. It was not there. I said, *I am going to take my life*, and for the first time, I heard a voice speak back to me, that sounded like me, but very grounded and wise.

The conversation went a lot like this:

I am going to take my life.
Take your life where?

I want to die.
Do you really? Or what part of you or your life do you want to die?

What's the point?
Well, what IS the point? Tell me, I am listening.

I don't know, I've had enough.
What have you had enough of?

I've had enough of this pain.
Well, do something with it then.

Like what?
What do you feel?

Like a rotten apple that's been left in the sun in a bowl that no-one picks and it's only going to keep rotting away and affect all the other fruit.

What if you're not just the apple and you're the entire bowl and all the fruits in it? What if your pain is the apple? What might the other fruits represent? Love? Joy? Creativity?

Well, I don't want those parts to die …
So, what part of you is this rotten apple?

This placement, it's sucking the life out of me.
So how about you leave the placement rather than Earth?

But what if I still feel the pain?
You probably will feel a pain, but not the same one. Let's have this discussion again then though, you have to trust me.

Trust you? You're the one that got me into this mess!
Well, let's clean it up huh?

I hate cleaning.
What do you hate more? Cleaning or leaving a mess for other people to clean up?

Well damn. Fine.

I opened my eyes and there was a sense of calmness in the air. I sent that email. I put the medication back into the cupboard, got my backpack, locked up the house and walked to the nearest bus stop. Side note: Aqua had a new carer there within half an hour. I felt completely numb and like a robot until the bus turned up. I suddenly felt the breeze on my face. It felt like it stood me up and pushed me onto that bus. As I sat down a wave of relief washed over me, and I felt like I had just woken up from an awful dream. Something did die that day. It was my care barometer. With little maintenance—self-care, connection, play—it was no longer able to tell me that my care battery was empty and that it had completely fried itself. As I sat on that bus, I felt a sensation grow that I hadn't felt in a long time. I closed my eyes and there was the speckle of light behind my eyelids and a small buzz of energy in my belly. I opened my eyes to make sure I wasn't dreaming, and a smile formed on my face. It had been so long since I had smiled, that it physically hurt my cheeks.

The conversation with my other self, continued on that bus ride and I concluded that the other fruits could handle being near the apple, only if I'm eating them and replacing them all quickly enough, so none of them could rot. I need to eat the love, joy and creativity regularly. The apple originally was being a carer, but by only eating apples, I wasn't getting all the nutrients I needed. I became tired and I was rotting away.

•

With time, when I would acknowledge my experiences, was when I received the gifts. I realised that:

- I matter most.
- I was given a brand spanking new care barometer and by getting on that bus, it had started to charge up my care battery, for myself.
- That sometimes, things have to die to be able to start again.
- That the other me, was perhaps the higher self that people had talked about, and she had just saved my life. And where did I find her? In the absolute dark, the void, the abyss—deep within my body, my being.
- The dark is where I found clarity and answers. It isn't to be feared. There is ultimate potential in this place.

I stayed in this chrysalis for many years. I know, because despite these gifts presenting themselves, I was still in an immense amount of emotional pain and mental torment. I had no idea how to care for myself or to move beyond some of my pains.

I was quite determined though, to stay and find another placement, but to enforce more boundaries. You guessed it, I crashed and burned again. While it was definitely the best placement yet, I was completely burnt out. People have told me that I was experiencing trauma, compassion fatigue and was in a dark night of the soul. I decided to embrace the feeling of failing and moved back home.

•

When I came home, I went and lived with my dad in a new town, as I couldn't bring myself to live in my hometown. It felt like I couldn't face the hundreds of people who I knew before. The person who came back was not the person who had left, and I didn't know how to integrate. I wanted to avoid the 'Oh my goodness, how was overseas?' and I was too tired to lie and say it was amazing. I was also too scared to say the truth, that I thought about not wanting to be alive anymore, every day for eight months. I hid in my dad's basement. I told no one the reality of my inner world. I gave hints about my experiences, in hope that would be enough for them to understand why I wasn't the chirpy-happy-April. Sure, they affirmed these experiences were horrible, but no one asked me how I *really* was or whether I needed help to process, and that made me feel just as alone. I eventually acknowledged that people aren't mind readers, it was my responsibility to voice my truth. But I didn't and suffered in this silence. I think my dad recognised suffering, so did things with me in his own way to try and help.
✷ He gave me my own space, some work, juice fasts, water fasts, cooked some meals, and listened to whatever I did have the courage to say. I felt small shifts in my mood and my empty tank

Pain as a Portal

slowly being refuelled, but the intrusive thoughts didn't stop. I can remember there came a point where they changed though. They went from feeling heavy, charged with a uselessness and exhausted tone, void of hope, to being more childlike and lighter, with flickers of hope, wonder and possibilities in the questions. The conversations started looking a bit like this:

I want to take my life...
  Take your life where?

To go back overseas to experience it and NO WORK this time. I do have tickets to go to Tomorrowland, but I don't want my friends seeing me like this. I'll be a burden.
  Yeah, you're right, cancel...

But... Tomorrowland, the land of tomorrow sounds promising. It's certainly a place I'd like to take my life, into tomorrow.
  Oh, would it now? So, you don't want to die?

Well, there must be more to life than this...
  So... you've got tickets booked to Tomorrowland, you're going with friends who have the words cope, more and Christ in their names. How many more signs do you bloody need?

•

So, I did. In July 2013, I went on the trip. If I am completely honest, in the back of my head was also the voice, *It's easier to disappear over there.* So, that made it easier. The plane ride over was filled with flashbacks and a mighty panic attack. Thankfully, I had a row to myself and everyone else was asleep. The following part is a haze in my memory. To this day I am unsure of whether this was a dream or whether it happened. So, for the sake of truth, let's say it was a dream.

✸ While I thought I was a master of being unseen, one of the flight attendants sat down next to me and asked if I was okay. I responded by asking what her definition of okay was. She laughed and asked where I was headed and why. I could easily tell her where I was headed but when it came to the why, I froze. She said, 'Ah, not for business huh. If it's not for business, the why always stumps people. I do suggest you work out your why, so you have an easier road to recognising it when you find it. Discovering the why along the way can be more painful. Both get there though.'

I woke up. Metaphorically or literally, I do not know, but let's go with both. Boy did that change the rest of the flight. My favourite concept, *why*. After much deliberation I decided my why was to find answers to the questions that I have found intrusive and frankly disturbing over the last year.

First, I did some exploring by myself, because I was not ready to be around my old best mate. He would know for sure that something was up, he always did. I always hated and absolutely loved his ability to really see through my smile that I showed the world.

✸ I started by attending a three-day music festival by myself, MELT in Germany. Okay MELT, what did I want to MELT away? Pain, so much fucking pain. And that, it did. Well, at least the top layer. I sat amongst the people. I danced. I sang. I didn't want to make friends, I was too tired, but I wanted to be around people and music. I discovered that feeling alone and lonely are very different feelings. Being alone was a strong desire because I still wasn't confident that I wouldn't let people walk all over me, along with not wanting to impact them with my pain.

I then met up with my mates in Belgium for Tomorrowland music festival, host of 180,000 attendees. Thankfully they were

Pain as a Portal

beaming with excitement, and I was a master of pretending to be happy, so my feelings flew under the radar. ✸ When I didn't want to go in the mosh, I told them to go ahead, that I was all good. One of them always stayed with me or at least close by. Being a killjoy was my worst nightmare but now that I was taking matters into my own hands, fun, crazy, mosh parts of April were put to rest for a few days. *People watching April*, took precedence. I took some MDMA, which numbed a lot of my emotional pain along with the physical pain of breaking my toe, all while reminding my system of what joy feels like, a bittersweet remembrance.

✸ After the festival, we parted ways and I headed to the next music festival Sziget, in Hungary. My body wanted to dance and explore, my thoughts and sore toe couldn't help themselves but to enjoy it.

My next destination was Portugal. I decided that along with my 30kg of luggage, that I would walk the last 100km of the Camino de Santiago up the west coast of Portugal into Spain. I went with a friend I had met on previous travels, who was my safety net because he spoke Spanish and Portuguese. We arrived at our starting point and quickly discovered that we had very different levels of fitness and the pace at which I walked was too frustrating for him, so we parted ways. Anxiousness started to set in but the yellow painted arrows on different parts of the streets and cheerful locals yelling, 'Buen Camino,' as you walked past, translating to 'Good Camino,' was very comforting.

After the first day of walking 22km, I was physically fatigued and in physical pain in every part of my body. When I reached the albergue (hostel), I entered the deepest sleep I can ever remember having. ✸ When I woke the next day, I found a hand-drawn picture on my chest, of a bag on a bus, a dotted line ending with an arrow, pointing to a bag at Santiago with an address. In panic, I looked around and could not find my bag anywhere except for my small bag with some of my belongings. My passport, phone and wallet was all there! Sidenote: it turns out that the recommended weight of the belongings you carry is 10% of your body weight. I started to become aware of my naivety of the intensity of the pilgrimage I had set out on and that I probably should have researched it better … or maybe not. The albergue was empty because everyone else had already set off for their next day of walking. There was nothing to do except trust, so I set off for the day.

✳ Along the way, a group of people rushed over to me signalling that they had given me the drawing. None of them could speak English. I was stunned at this beautiful act of kindness, so I tried my best to express my gratitude with the universal language of smiles, hugs and a very Australian accented 'Obrigado' which is 'Thank you' in Portuguese. The group stuck with me for the entire walk despite how slow, injured, and emotional I was. Occasionally, they insisted on taking turns carrying my bag and lending me their walking sticks for assistance. As I could not communicate verbally with them, or anyone for a week—I met no English-speaking people—I was initiated into again, the feeling of differentiating the difference between aloneness and loneliness. This was my mind speaking though. When I quieted the mind, neither was present. I was completely connected with the earth, the summer sun and the energy of the people I was with. If anything, it was an incredibly pure experience of their essence as I did not know their story, but I felt their kindness, love and their own pain they experienced from the walk. This was a rare and special experience, a gift indeed.

I embarked on this walk because someone told me I should. It wasn't until halfway through, that I remembered I needed to have my why aka my intention. ✳ I decided that my why was to shed the parts that hurt, to get to know myself better beyond the carer role and to let the mystery of life show me what it thought I needed. Well, it listened. The shedding had begun long before my conscious intention to shed had been initiated. My feet bled from blisters, my muscles ached, I sweated profusely, and I cried, a lot. I had often used the term 'slept like a log' throughout my life, but on this trip, I embodied the log like never before. Each night when I laid down, it felt like dawn rose in an instant and I was in the exact position I laid down in. Throughout the days when I wasn't experiencing physical pain, I was experiencing emotional pain.

There was a lot of space and time to contemplate, and with contemplation, came memories and an abundance of feelings. Every day, I could feel the pain shifting, changing, morphing and easing. More moments of peace, solitude, contentedness, joy, wonder and gratitude flooded by being. My prayers were being answered right before my eyes. *That* is who I was beyond the roles I played in life. I felt the presence of something greater than myself, something huge, something loving and powerful. Some call it Source, some call it God, but whatever name this presence goes by, there was no doubt in my being that it was there. I felt safe, watched over and a lightness that felt like magic, powerful, loving, indescribable magic.

PHASE 4

When we reached the destination point, the Santiago de Compostela Cathedral, I fell to the pavement in awe of my accomplishment and utter relief that it was over. Tears poured while cheers of joy and laughter from all the walkers reverberated around the cathedral square. We danced and sang and called our loved ones. Experiencing and witnessing this was one of the greatest gifts I have ever received. I reconnected with nature. I was reminded that humans can be good and pure. I realised that while caring for others is one of my strengths, I needed to care for myself just as much. I was confused but relieved that my emotional anguish felt much less intense and much more manageable. I felt light. I felt **hopeful** and excited to do life again. For the first time in a really long time, I couldn't wait to wake up the next day to see what the day had in store for me. This freedom from hopelessness lasted for weeks!

•

Returning home this time, I felt like I was coming back more myself than ever before. When I looked back at the darkest point, when I felt like I was losing myself, I had the clarity that I wasn't losing myself, I was losing or shedding the parts that no longer served me anymore. Every step, dance and tear was shedding the pain.

Nowadays, most days, I have conversations with people who are feeling as if they are drowning in the abyss or considering or planning to end their life. These conversations come forth from clients of all ages, friends, family and often strangers in the street.

Pain as a Portal

Often, just as the words have been freed from within, there is a mere moment in time, the space between their exhale and next inhale, that feels like the entire universe stops and takes a loving pause. They take their next deep inhale and, on the breath out they say they can't believe that they had just told me the truth of how they feel. There is often a glint of shock or regret on their face, soon followed by a sigh of relief to share the weight of the burden of this secret.

My personal experience has provided me with one of my most treasured gifts, the ability to listen, sit and speak with people from a place of reverence, love, honesty, truth and absolute trust of this experience. This cannot and does not come from a book or a degree, it comes straight from the place in my heart that not only spent time in these places but emerged out of them. To be trusted to hold loving space for people when they are at their most vulnerable state, is an indescribable honour.

✧

——————— Thank you pain. Thank you, gifts. ———————

✧

PORTAL PAINTINGS

☐ As I spun the wood slowly to create a spiral and then added the figures slowly descending to the centre, I started to feel dizzy. The effect of this slow spiralling to paint *'hopeless'* took me physically into the old feelings of descending into the dark. I had to close my eyes often, to centre myself, and oh how the dark feels different for me now. As the paint dried, I stared at it, while sipping some tea and reminisced about the many parts of myself that have been shed and absorbed by the Universe.

Writing these words and painting *'hopeful'* marked ten years since emerging from the chrysalis of hopelessness. Ten cycles around the sun feels like an empowering anniversary. To close my eyes and travel back to that dark, sticky time, with an evolved lens of sense of self, ignited the immense amount of self-compassion and hopefulness that was felt back at that time. It was bursting within me like fireworks. This, paired with words, colours and sound felt like my internal mother archetype paying tribute to my young, tender, fragile, maiden self.

❁

'hopeless'
as a portal to
'hopeful'

empathy as a portal to compassion

PHASE 1

I feel everything that is around me.
I always have.

PHASE 2

Daily, hourly

Empathy blurred the lines of what is mine and what is someone else's. I would meet people in their suffering and would give them all of me, to try and take their pain away. When they would leave, I would be so worried about them and so energetically drained, that I couldn't look after myself. I couldn't pull them out of their pain because I was then drowning in pain too. Note that when I say 'them', I am speaking of friends, family, clients, strangers, animals, plants, the earth and the human collective's suffering.

No wonder I want to take everyone's pain away, because that would be taking my pain away too.

Working in community services, I was constantly told not to 'take home' anything from work. This felt impossible, especially when 'home' was not only the house where I lived, but my mind, body and spirit.

PHASE 3

Approximately 30 years

✸ My mum has told me that as a child, I would relay my entire day to her when I got home from school, in detail. I would often talk about how the way people treated me and/or themselves affected me, mostly appearing confused, disappointed or worried. She witnessed me get it out of my system, very quickly seem unphased and I would carry on. She felt that at the time, as exhausting as this was for her to listen, that this was one of my intuitive magic keys to coping, processing, learning and moving through life, relatively unscathed. It would appear that she was right.

When I moved out of home however, I naively lost my key. I stopped expressing most of my experiences and kept them to myself. I had lots of internal conversations with myself, but this made them swim around inside me constantly. Eventually, they would burst out of me in the form of an emotional meltdown which always felt unexpected and unreasonable for what I was currently experiencing.

My Portals

On a few occasions, a big cry and a day in bed didn't express my feelings nearly enough. I felt severely fatigued and found it difficult to experience joy. I would carry on as per normal regardless, which only ever resulted in my body becoming more tired, numb and miserable, to the point of *having* to stop and slow down, instead of *choosing* to. When this happened, it took months to feel back to my baseline energy levels and often involved experiencing a physical illness.

•

This pattern continued relentlessly until 2022, the year I will forever remember as when *'pain as a portal'* showed up in my life. For that entire year, I practiced being more intentional with my time and my energy. I now know that tiredness serves as a kind friend, reminding me to slow down and to reevaluate where I am sending my energy. I continuously practiced noticing a pain, naming it and expressing it intentionally. ☐ I did this daily, sometimes hourly, especially on the days where my role at work was to hold space for other people's pain. In between therapy sessions I would do my best to have a dance, jump up and down, shake and jiggle, scream, breathe slowly, stretch, journal or ask the sun to dissolve the pains with its rays.

•

No-human-Sundays became a weekly practice, with the intention being to give myself space instead of others and to rejuvenate, integrate and regulate. I still do this, to this day. It's called practice for a reason though. Sometimes, I forget. Sometimes, I intentionally

Pain as a Portal

choose to engage with people, making a judgment call that it will serve my intention to rejuvenate, just in a different way to solitude.

PHASE 4

To know in my bones that pain can be a portal to a gift, I am invited to meet people in their pain, but not sink with them. Their pain is not mine. I will be gifted with enough pain of my own. The idea of taking away people's pain feels like the ultimate disservice, as I would be taking away a gift that they so deeply deserve for all they have been through.

When meeting people while they are suffering, I want to lovingly wade by them, as they intentionally dive into the well of their pain. As they come up for air, to release and express this pain in whatever way feels true to them, I breathe lightly and gently, so their breath can match mine. When I speak, their body listens and it feels the frequency that ripples through the air, of trust and knowing, that this suffering they are in right now, holds a gift waiting to show itself. My voice holds patience, for I know this pain must be felt and their soul knows for how long. It holds compassion for I know too, what it feels like to suffer and to be filled to the brim with pain. I try my best to emanate the room with love, for I know love is pain's favoured environment to morph into a gift. While I do not say these words to them out loud, this is the multilayered message I am sending when their mind hears me say, 'Tell me more' or 'I hear you' or 'Show me with colour'.

This does not mean that I wish pain or suffering upon anyone or find any enjoyment in it. While it is freeing to burst out of my chrysalis, with wings that no longer hold the weight of trying to take all of someone's pain away or save them from it, I still find witnessing suffering painful. What has shifted for me by applying 'pain as a portal' to my life, is that this pain of empathy lasts for mere minutes before it is transformed into connection, relating, relationship, patience, **compassion** and love. I am deeply grateful for these gifts, and I will willingly dive into this portal again and again and again, because every time I do, I come closer and closer to meeting and being my truest self.

◆

———————— Thank you pain. Thank you, gifts. ————————

◆

PORTAL PAINTINGS

☐ Painting *'empathy'* and *'compassion'* felt very comfortable to create. These feelings are close to the surface of my being, always. The day afterwards however, I was presented with the physical sensation of heaviness in my body that I wanted to escape from.
☐ My monthly therapy session thankfully fell on this day, where I was supported by going into these sensations somatically and seeing what they had to tell me. It became apparent that I had opened my portal of empathy, to the world's suffering. I felt suffocated by it and scared. With breath, movement and visualising a giant 'negative energy vacuum' sucking up the darkness and spitting it into a black hole, I felt peace again. I directed some love and attention into the compassion side of the painting, to intentionally close this portal.

'empathy'
as a portal to
'compassion'

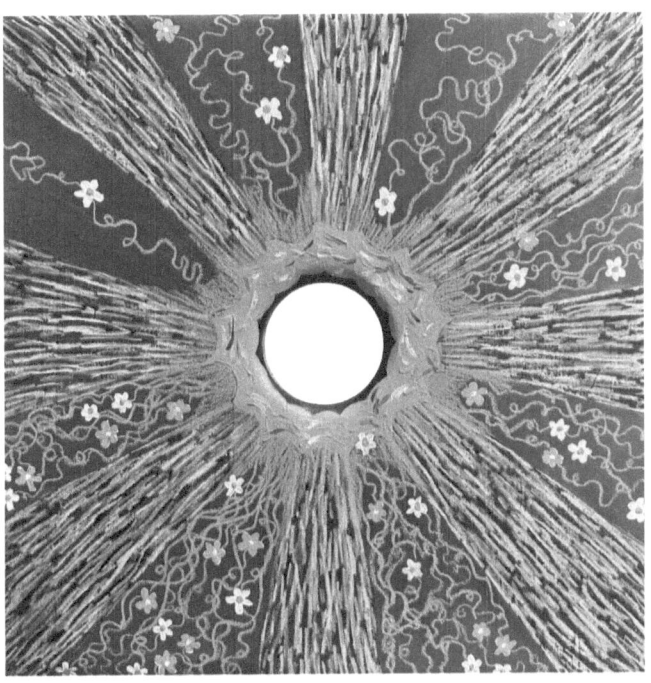

violated as a *portal* to forgiveness

PHASE 1

I was sexually assaulted by someone I called a friend.

PHASE 2

My body moved through many sensations that night. Shock. Guilt. Fear. Numbness. Confusion. Fragile. Frozen. Fatigue. **Violated**.

Pain as a Portal

PHASE 3

Approximately 8 years

I felt an immediate shift in my sense of reality. The colours of the world dulled. Sounds muffled. My spirit went into hiding. So, did I. My body was suddenly void of feeling. I made every excuse possible to explain his actions, as I wanted to be wrong. I blamed myself, talked myself into believing it wasn't what I thought. I entered a void of denial. I stayed friends with him, carried on like nothing had happened. So did he. I told no-one.

•

A few months afterwards, I felt the call to go to Nepal. During the three-month visit, I had some of my most impactful experiences to date. I volunteered in an orphanage and taught English to women. I did a seven-day trek to Ghorepani Poon Hill, a popular viewpoint of the Annapurna mountain ranges. I volunteered at a vulture conservation camp and went parahawking with Bob, the Egyptian Vulture.

☐ The ten-day Silent Vipassana Retreat was one of those experiences that felt like I stepped in as one person and left as another. Vipassana means 'to see things as they really are' and it certainly lived up to its meaning. This retreat consisted of ten days of silence. No speaking, no eye contact, no consuming animal products, or touching, using technology, pens or books. Females and males were separated. All of these rules were set with the intention to limit distraction. The only things available to consume were light vegetarian meals, occasional walks in the fresh air, sleep, your thoughts and sensations. Hundreds of us sat for ten hours a day in meditation, learning the Vipassana practice.

You are told that you will experience what you need to and that there is no single outcome of this experience. I personally came to understand a new level of physical discomfort. I experienced excruciating physical pain and unbearable sensations in my body intermittently. The practice teaches us to acknowledge pain, without judgement and to return to the practice of scanning our bodies with intentional attention. Despite being given this clear instruction, I wrapped myself in blankets and squirmed for the first six days, trying to get comfortable and lessen the pain. My mind would distract me with thoughts, like what type of dog I wanted, taking my attention away from my body. This is when the pain would strike.

Part way through day six, like the flick of a light switch, my mind and my body began cooperating. Once I surrendered to the pain, acknowledged it with no judgment and returned to putting my attention on other parts of my body, I physically felt the pain dissipate, immediately. The pain would continue to rise and leave, rise and leave. This process became quicker and quicker and for the last four days, I predominately felt timeless, weightless, peaceful and full of grace.

Soon after the Vipassana retreat, I went home. Despite trying to continue my practice in a typical environment, I was quickly sucked back into the vortex of living by time and being busy at work. Soon, I had completely neglected my practice. I had re-entered the realms of my mind, disconnecting again from my body.

•

Pain as a Portal

I am sure that it comes to no surprise that I engaged in a lot of work and an on and off relationship with a guy who repeatedly took advantage of my naive, trusting and compassionate nature. I had decided the relationship was as good as it was going to get, and that I preferred occasional pleasurable times over being alone. Despite my insatiable appetite for literature about the psychology of human behaviour, it took many years for me to apply my knowledge to my own circumstances. It is noteworthy that whenever I was with this person, the friend, from the aforementioned incident, would drift out of the picture. I have come to know that my body's intelligence is beyond what is imaginable and always has me in its best interests, so I have concluded that it is very likely that this is one of the unconscious reasons why I stayed in this partnership. More on this in the next chapter.

•

✷ I started studying Sandplay Therapy. More on that specifically in a later chapter, too. This was where I learned the works of Carl Jung, the unconscious, the shadow, symbolism and much more. My teacher believed strongly in intention. Over the next few years, I started to notice that everywhere I turned, living intentionally was encouraged, so I surrendered to practicing being more intentional with all aspects of my life, to see what would happen. As you have discovered, I was quickly converted.

•

☐ One of my friends was learning the art of Womb Rebozo Massage and put out a call looking for people to practice on. My being screamed a resounding 'yes'. I met her weekly for a month, with the intention to dedicate this time to work on the 'black void' and 'abyss' that I felt in my womb space. When I placed my attention in this space, it felt like never ending darkness with no beginning or end, filled with guilt, fear, shame and grief.

She massaged only the womb space, inclusive of my stomach and lower back. To finish, she wrapped me up in material and gently rocked me. Tears rolled down my cheeks as I realised, she had been giving me and my hurt more genuine love and care than I ever have. She finished by leaving me tightly wrapped in the material for about ten minutes, to allow the experience to settle within my body. I felt like I was inside a chrysalis, safe and warm. I loved it. Memories, emotions, visions and realisations rose to the surface. This regular meeting assisted to transform my inner scary abyss into a cosmos of potential and grounding.

•

During this phase, my intentional creative expression was typically intended to shift emotions that I thought were related to *other* experiences. Often, they would bring me simultaneously back to the pain of *this* experience. Little earthquakes happened throughout my body, cracking me open, bringing feeling back to the surface.

Over a few years, I had met with all of the feeling friends that my body had been carrying for years underneath the numbness. Clarity. Rage. Shame. Humiliation. Revolt. Anger. Violation. Anxious. Fearful. Overwhelmed. Disrespected. Confused. Distant. Nauseated. Dirty. Sticky. Dense.

Pain as a Portal

☐ Through the combination of therapy, study, art, dance, breaking up with a guy, spending a year alone, and entering the most loving and respectful relationship to date, I was ready to dive into the reality of what my numbness was in response to. I finally started to see clearly. Acceptance landed and courage rose in my body.

When I started being honest with myself and those closest to me, it became apparent that my numbness had started long before the incident with my friend. The memory of being stalked on my walk home when I was in primary school came to mind and body. Then, the memory of a male at a party, post high school, who did not respect my no and despite me fighting, he got his way. On this occasion, a few friends didn't believe me, so I kept that to myself for a long time. From all of these experiences, I had made the unconscious decision that I didn't feel safe in my body and that it was much safer to be in my mind. It felt like the previous experiences were nothing compared to the agony I was now feeling. There was something different about it being someone I knew, someone that I called a friend. There was trust broken and boundaries disrespected in many ways over those years. When this became apparent, there was an undeniable knowing within me that I had to cease contact with him. It took me a little while, with multiple attempts, but I did. Panic attacks started to lessen, I lost some excess weight, and a sense of freedom came occasionally. Fear, anxiety, paranoia and guilt stuck by me for up to a year however, so I knew that this experience and person still had hold of me.

•

☐ One day while meditating on a beach, I sat with an intention: To free myself from what no longer serves me.

My meditation showed a snake that asked to enter me. Its energy felt pure, so I allowed it. It entered through my yoni, with its length reaching to the top of my spine. It then started to spin so fast that it was a tube of light. Dark, dense, sticky black energy within me started being purified by this light. It felt like emotional residue was being eradicated. Then with a final flash of light, it rocketed out the top of my head. As I opened my eyes and came back to my bodily senses, the most spectacular rainbow adorned the sky. I knew that what felt like residue of him and others within my body, had been eradicated. I felt lighter, cleaner.

•

☐ Sometimes, I get strong urges to stop what I am doing and tend to pain. Sometimes, the timing doesn't suit as these urges can rise while I'm at work, in the supermarket or with a friend. On this day, the urge was insistent, so I made space in my schedule to inquire. I felt compelled to contemplate, meditate, and dance with my shadow, which led me to ask to be shown the part of me where mistreatment of another is born. The many ways that I mistreat myself started flooding to mind, along with the realisation that every time I have mistreated myself, or others, I had been experiencing a considerable amount of pain. On a day not too long after, I danced with my rage. I was fuelled with a fiery energy and a voice that told me to hurt him to get my power back. I was suddenly scared and ashamed that I had this thought, and my dance quickly formed into panic and loss of breath. It suddenly dawned on me that actions of mistreatment are often a response to a perceived loss of power, and loss of power is usually a response to intense pain or mistreatment. I spoke to my inner power and practiced connecting to it, increasing it, and decreasing it. I realised that power is life itself, so power resides within me. The loss of power was a mere concept of my mind. So, to play along, I imagined taking my power back and putting it back in my body. My heart throbbed, sending me the message of what an immense amount of pain someone must be in, to act in such a way. I was then filled with compassion for him, then myself, then those I have either intentionally or unintentionally hurt. I wept while hugging myself, pleading for forgiveness from all. Suddenly without thought, I started apologising to my body. *I am so sorry for not listening to you when you were trying to tell me something. I am so sorry for blaming you, it wasn't your fault. You did not deserve this. I am sorry for mistreating you all this time by neglecting you. I am sorry for not protecting you. I am sorry for not having stronger boundaries to keep you safe.*

The tears stopped and my body felt like a blanket of peace had been placed over it. My heart said, *I forgive you.* My body was buzzing with ecstatic love.

After a moment of pure bliss, I decided that forgiveness was a key to my emotional freedom. I sat in prayer, forgiving all the people that had intentionally or unintentionally mistreated me. I acknowledged I was not condoning their actions, however sending love to their pain. I forgave myself and made a vow, to try my very best to treat all—including myself—from a place of love.

•

I became very interested in intergenerational wounds. It became apparent that along my maternal and paternal lines, was a prevalent theme of abuse of all kinds, with both perpetrators and victims on both sides. Among my family members there was naturally a cacophony of varying responses, all as an attempt to cope with the mistreatment. Repression and suppression of emotion and silencing the voice seemed to be the ones I took on and were deeply embedded in my psyche. This played out in many ways and areas of my life. I was now determined to actively break these patterns through intentional creative expression.

☐ Due to these patterns living within me on a cellular level, I decided to mark this intention by receiving a therapeutic tattoo. Marking my skin by intentional tattooing has been and continues to be, one of my most potent acts to intentionally and creatively express and honour myself. On this occasion, my intention was to receive shoulder tattoos that symbolised protection, so that the cells in my body knew that I was safe.

☐ Over the coming months, as the intention of the tattoos settled in my body, my shoulders started to feel heavier. Over my lifetime, caving my shoulders inwards was an unconscious habit of trying to be small, but my partner always encouraged me to stand tall and to own my space. Practicing this brought a lot of confidence to my state of mind and a greater sense of personal power. The new heaviness of my shoulders was pulling them forward, which was contradicting their intention. They felt like armour. I contemplated the initial intention, closed my eyes, and asked my body how it felt when I told it. *You are protected, you are safe.* I immediately felt fearful, wanting to open my eyes, to check for potential danger. I contemplated that potential risk is a part of life, so what would make me feel more empowered within my body? The words, *I am supported*, flew into my mind like a carrier pigeon had just dropped the message. I asked my body how this felt and immediately my shoulders felt lighter, they stood tall, my spine straightened, and I felt powerful. The support of the Universe, my fire within and the people closest to me, felt present. I thanked the affirmation of *I am safe* for serving its purpose up until this time and welcomed my new truth statement of *I am supported* into my shoulders and body.

•

Slowly over time I felt the energetic threads that were connecting me to the people who have mistreated me, become less like chains, and more like a single strand of spider silk that with one strong breath, I could snap. ☐ When memories rose, I sent the memories love, the people love and myself love.

PHASE 4

The realisation that I had emerged from this chrysalis came about unexpectedly, when it dawned on me that I felt no discomfort in my body when I thought about the people associated with experiences of sexual, physical and psychological mistreatment or the experiences themselves. There was no anxiety. No panic. No rage. No fear. I felt neutral. I felt *forgiveness*. I didn't have to intentionally send love anywhere, I felt it, reverberating in my heart space.

    I knew for sure that this was the case, when writing this chapter. I shed tears of pride, self-compassion, gratitude and relief that there was finally peace inside my body.

✧

———— Thank you pain. Thank you, gifts. ————

✧

My Portals

PORTAL PAINTINGS

☐ I was met with some resistance for the painting of *'violated'*. I discovered that compared to the others I had done so far, it was particularly hard to paint this pain, as it didn't feel alive and at the surface. My body wasn't sure that it wanted to dive into this sensation of violation. What I do know though, is how repressed emotion is a very sneaky friend who likes to play hide and seek, so I made myself a cup of tea, put on a snuggly jumper and reminded my body that the intention of this process was to release any residue that I may have previously missed, *not* to re-enter into this sensation, for the sake of a story. Colours started to catch my attention and once I put my thoughts aside and made the first brush stroke, it painted itself. I experienced a lot of discomfort by looking at what was being created, as the texture of the paint ignited old feelings, yet it was empowering to honour and release.

Fears of what people who read this may think or say started to enter my mind. Would they believe me? Would they reject me? Would they twist what I have said into their own version? What if I am questioned for further details? As I started to feel my thoughts spiral, I imagined sending these thoughts and fears into the painting because what people say, think or do is out of my control and none of my business.

It dawned on me that once solid trust was built with my new boyfriend, it was love that made me brave enough to put up all boundaries required. Being single, paired with a lack of self-love, made me feel vulnerable, alone and scared in the world. When with those who mistreated me, my mind created scenarios of all their potential reactions to me choosing to leave, so it unconsciously felt safer to keep them close. The clarity of the complexity of humans and human relationships (functional or dysfunctional) eased a lot of my self-judgement of how confusing my actions may appear to others.

Self-compassion assisted in painting *forgiveness*. These feelings were definitely working closely together to get me through this time.

'violated'
as a portal to
'forgiveness'

insecure as a portal to love

Note:
This portal and the previous portal of violation
were very tightly intertwined in time,
my body and mind …

PHASE 1

Early 20s

I was at the pub, moderately intoxicated by alcohol and excitement. A guy approached me and immediately, we had a strong connection.

Pain as a Portal

PHASE 2

I entered into a monogamous relationship with said guy. I felt *insecure*, fat, ugly, undesirable and like I wanted to hide my body and soul long before he came along. His unexpected attention subsided these feelings, momentarily. I very quickly started to feel doubt and that something didn't feel right, but I wasn't quite sure how to read that feeling, so my inner critical voice would take over and tell me things like, *Don't overthink it, just enjoy it. You're so boring, just have fun. You're lucky to be getting any attention at all.* I listened to that voice a lot.

Our relationship had many moments of joy, playfulness and excitement too, which is what made me doubt my internal gut feeling. 'The feeling' however, would visit often and I would continue to shut it down.

PHASE 3

4+ years

He would tell me he loved me, that he was monogamous, loyal and happy and that I ticked all his boxes. Every so often I could hear the words but couldn't feel them, so I would try and talk myself into believing him. Sometimes it worked, but suspicion and doubt always returned. I became aware of his infidelity, only to be told I was imagining things when I would broach the subject. My previous boyfriend did the same, so I started to wonder why I wasn't enough. I talked myself into believing everything he told me about myself, which often reinforced my feelings of insecurity.

I did everything he told me to do. I became more isolated. I spent less time with my friends and any time when I wasn't at work, was with him. My self-worth diminished over time. The thing that kept me hooked, was repeatedly telling myself that this was as good as it's going to get, along with having a strong playful and sexual connection. I felt safe sexually with him. He always respected my no and my desired pace. After previously unpleasant sexual experiences, I valued this over all other aspects of my well-being. Eventually, something big enough would happen and I would break up with him, only to forgive and get back together multiple times.

•

During this time, I was working as a support worker for people with disabilities. I became passionate about working specifically with people who were non-verbal, with a special interest in finding ways for them to express their needs or wants without the need for speech. One day, I was sitting on my best friend's couch when I Googled: Therapies for non-verbal people. Sandplay Therapy caught my attention. I rang a company that did the certification, and they had one spot left in their training, which would be in a few weeks' time. I had a sense of it's meant to be, so I booked in. Days before leaving I developed a chest infection, which wasn't uncommon, however this time it developed into pneumonia. ✱ When I rang to cancel, the man on the other end of the phone said, 'Illness is a message, we will keep your place if you can come to another city instead, it sounds like you need this course.' I couldn't shake his comment. It was the first time I had heard someone link a physical illness to a message.

I went to the face-to-face training every few months over the

Pain as a Portal

next few years. What I learned about myself, Jungian psychology, human behaviour, emotional wounds, boundaries, belief systems and symbology broke my heart open over and over again, allowing the hurt to pour out to then be mended with love, understanding, empowerment and resolve. Thankfully, part of the Sandplay Therapy training included being a participant in therapy. I had never received any counselling or therapy previously. It was overwhelming. I felt vulnerable and raw, yet held and supported. There was a lot to unpack. Many realisations about recurring patterns that played out in my life came to light. One in particular that stood out, was my recurring chest infections. ☐ I was encouraged to look closely at the emotional pain alongside the physical pain. I felt voiceless, breathless, constricted, scared and cold. My trainer asked me what it was that I wanted to say, without holding back. 'I want to leave,' flew out of my mouth. Looking back on every time I got this infection, there was a situation I wanted to leave, but stayed. A relationship, a job, another relationship, another job, a house, another relationship, another job.

Since becoming aware of this pattern, when the crackle in my back starts, I thank it and look at my life and where I need to ascertain a boundary or walk away from something. I now action this, before the infection takes control. I also realised that I felt at home with non-verbal people because I too, metaphorically, did not speak my truth.

•

As for the relationship with my boyfriend, the chest infection wasn't enough. It took one of the girls he was having an affair with, to physically assault me, for me to wake up to the reality of what I was living. He refused to be a witness when I reported her. I was fired up with the electric energy of certainty throughout my body, that this was it. I ended the relationship, for the last time. My boundary was not respected and there was endless attempts of contact and reconnection, despite my lack of response.

After experiencing a period of fearing the girl who assaulted me, an overwhelming amount of gratitude for her actions filled my being. She literally knocked sense into me. I was finally free. I finally had the emotional space to look at what I had experienced in this relationship and all of my relationships, with men, friends, family, workmates and community members.

•

✷ I got a dog. The exact dog that I imagined whilst in Vipassana. White, small, fluffy, Morris. He was a gift, every hour, every day, in many ways. The amount of love I felt for this little Maltese Terrier was a love I had never experienced before. My heart felt like it was bursting open simply by watching him. The content feeling that reverberated through my body whilst stroking his fur, put me under a spell. Morris reconnected me to a part of myself that had gone into hibernation. He quickly became a king, as I felt unconditionally in debt to him and the joy he brought to my life. As I write this, I cannot help but laugh as this created some not so pleasing behaviours for later in his doggy life. As it turns out, I am indeed meant to act like the master. To be honest, I am still learning how to do this, as to this day I want to pamper him with my gratitude.

•

Pain as a Portal

While The PAIN Process was not yet in my world in a clear systematic way, living intentionally and expressing myself creatively was. ☐ I embarked on what ended up being nicknamed the Year of April. I committed to getting to know myself better, remembering who I was at my core, working on my boundaries, tending to the emotional wounds that lived deep rooted in my body and mind and ceasing any sexual relationships until I trusted myself to choose a loving relationship. I started to play with manifestation and visualising the life I wanted. I visualised and journalled about the type of partner I wanted, but more importantly, how I wanted to feel when I was with them and what they valued.

•

✷ I developed my dearest friendship with someone who is without doubt, my soul-sister. We lived so close to each other that we saw each other most days. She was and is, one of my most treasured gifts of this lifetime. Kind and compassionate beyond comprehension, hilarious, supportive, fun and every attribute I appreciate in a friend. During the many challenging times in my life, I have been lovingly held by her and I honestly have no idea how I would have coped with life, without her.

•

This was a slow and pain-ridden year, as I continued my old patterns of over-working as a distraction and exhibiting my inability to say no to company requests, let alone the requests of family and friends. The chest infection arrived again. I knew I had to leave my job as a Service Manager in a disability company. I knew that

Sandplay Therapy was where my heart and soul were enriched, excited and courageous. I was filled with fear, but my love for Sandplay overrode fear. I quit. The relief was unexplainable.

There was something else to leave too though. The friendship from the previous chapter.

•

Alongside heartache, was heartthrob. There was a man that also worked for the disability company who always gave me butterflies. I never acted on them as we both lived our own lives. I knew very little about him, but he seemed happy in his world. Not long before leaving my job, he was newly single. My low self-esteem was still very present, so my mind was filled with thoughts of *He'd never go for you*. One of my best friends however affirmed me and built me up with the courage to initiate getting to know each other better. So, I invited him to a house party. ✻ We have been together since.

•

Being in a new partnership, awoke the dormant feelings of insecurity, suspicion, self-doubt, low self-esteem and distrust in authenticity. These feelings took a few years to diminish. They required therapy, paintings and many intentional letting go techniques. When these feelings would rise and I would say them out loud, my boyfriend would infuse them with love, in his many ways. He was so patient, which gave me permission to be patient with myself.

Pain as a Portal

☐ I did not want all that I had learned about myself to dissipate within the relationship, so I decided to have a Self-Marriage Ceremony. I had a ring tattooed on my left ring finger, symbolising my commitment to myself, first always. I wrote the following vows:

I vow;
to care for you when you are in pain
like I would a child or friend;
to listen to the inner knowing
that is clear and loud within;
to rejoice in the joys
as there are many;
to be courageous, patient and trusting
as we have chosen this time for a reason;
to allow your inner radiance
express itself fearlessly;
and to love you
with unwavering reverence.

Above this ring, I also got a dot tattooed. This dot symbolises my boyfriend. It symbolises that not only am I committed to him, to love him to the best of my ability, but that he is a daily a reminder that love, the way I dreamed of experiencing, is possible. It still amazes me that he is everything that I had yearned for, visualised and journalled about months prior.

PHASE 4

An emergence crept in slowly. There was no big moment. It was a slow realisation of how secure I felt in my new partnership and the abundance of *love* in my life, in many forms.

Now, when I think of my past relationship, I am free from any animosity or unpleasant sensations in my body. That relationship served me lessons, and for that I am grateful. I can smile at what I appreciated without adding a but, to the same thought, to negate them.

With my now boyfriend, I have never felt this kind of love before. It changes, flows and flourishes into things that continue to surprise me. Over our six years and counting, pain has of course met us fleetingly, but so far has only led to deeper, more cherished love. His love for me, my love for him, and our love combined makes me feel courageous, brave, loved and peaceful. This love created a sense of safety and security for me to burst free from not only *this* chrysalis, but many. His name means light-giving and he certainly lives up to his name. It is no wonder that he feels like home.

Love was also gifted in many friendships. Some have naturally drifted into different directions while others have strengthened and blossomed.

Self-love was also another gift. This one is still a work in progress, but on the days where self-love is present, life is sublime.

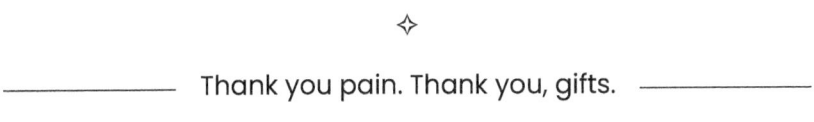

———— Thank you pain. Thank you, gifts. ————

PORTAL PAINTINGS

☐ Painting the feeling of *'insecure'* felt icky. I reflected on how feeling insecure appears to be some kind of rite of passage for teenagers, but that some people never come out the other side. For a while, I felt like I had been transported back there and I had to remind myself that it was only a painting of the past and that this grief for my younger self soon got to paint the gift of love.

Painting *'love'* was a gift in itself. The sheer amount of joy, ecstasy and appreciation that danced within my body was overwhelming. I couldn't physically paint this accurately. I had to cry happy tears, sing, dance, laugh, spin and skip to cope with the magnitude of this feeling.

❦

'insecure'
as a portal to
'love'

grief as a portal to soul connection

PHASE 1

Early 30's

My friend died. He was also a relative, but most importantly, my friend.

PHASE 2

He had a terminal illness, so we were anticipating his departure, however nothing prepared me for the feeling of ***grief*** that resided and ached in my heart for a long time after his death. I questioned life and became full of rage at the Universe for taking one of the kind and impactful ones, not only from me, but from my family, friends and community. I could not make any sense of it. Life began to feel nonsensical. In the same breath, I also felt a sense of relief, trusting that he was no longer in any pain.

PHASE 3

Approximately 4 months

I was devoted to expressing my pains through intentional creative expression during this time. I often wonder what state I would have been in if I didn't have this process to lean on.

My friend's funeral was beautiful. So many lovely people were there, also hurting, to share the pain and meet each other in loving embraces and to say all the words that wouldn't even begin to express the ache. As soon as the ceremony finished, my body went into a stress response. Panic rose and I had to flee. I couldn't contain the floodwaters. ☐ I fled and spent the afternoon sobbing and staring up to the sky. Thoughts ceased and numbness took over my body. While a funeral offers part of the processing of the concept of death, it certainly did not offer the complete closure I needed.

•

Everywhere I went reminded me of him. ☐ I left my teardrops in parks, shopping centres, my car, down my boyfriend's shirt, in river currents and over my journal pages as I honoured him and this sadness. I wore socks with his brand on it for too many days between washes, as I clenched onto him. I yearned to hug him, to see his cheeky, radiant grin, just one more time.

My Portals

The first time that the reminder of our regular scheduled morning tea catchup pinged on my phone calendar, felt like my heart fell out of my chest and shattered all over the ground. ☐ I still went, only this time, without him. I ordered what we always ordered and sobbed in the courtyard, where we always sat. Allowing this much emotion to flow in public felt embarrassing, but the importance of honouring such a beautiful human through my grief overpowered it. Staff at the coffee shop offered hugs, that spoke of their love and condolences and insisted that the order was on the house. If I had stayed home that day and suffered alone, I would not have been gifted the feeling of being so held by my community.

•

I felt so sad, that I was too tired to dance, paint, write or sing. ☐ All I could muster was to have baths, crying and telling my heart there was just a little more to release.

☐ One night, I sat in meditation pleading to see him. In the darkness behind my eyelids and in outer space, I waited and waited. Just as I was about to give up, all I could see was a bright orb buzzing around playfully. I knew straight away that it was him. It felt cheeky, loving and excitable, so I knew. I reminded him of how loved he was and how much I missed him. I thanked him for being unapologetically himself, wherever he went. I told him that I suspected that his business name Show Us Your Crack, was indeed a fabulous play on words for a phone repair business, but that perhaps it was also his way to subconsciously allow people to show their emotional cracks. He was always available to anyone and everyone, non-judgementally. He laughed and reminded me that it was now my turn, to show my cracks, to lead by example, so others were less afraid to show theirs. He then reminded me that he was still available, more than ever, to connect with if I ever needed.

I felt comforted by him and a sense of connectedness. I felt my Sandplay Teacher, Nan, Aunty and various other people who had crossed over that I wasn't even particularly close to. I felt surrounded by peace and a resounding message that *We're here.*

As I brought my awareness back into my body and opened my eyes, the intensity of the pain had completely subsided. There was calm.

Sometimes I wonder whether what I experience during meditation is my imagination, but mostly, I don't care 'what' it is. This meditation brought an immense amount of comfort and a sense of bravery that has stuck with me, as I embark on sharing my cracks with the world.

PHASE 4

Along with peace, it felt like my connection to the people who had crossed over was stronger. I could feel their purity, their wise self, their essence free from pain, masks or human conditioning, their soul if you will. I felt closer to them than ever before.

It's been a few years now, and the pain is different. I miss my friend exceptionally, but now I interpret this missing as him pulling on a magical invisible string that connects our hearts as a reminder to connect with him. The missing comes with a smile. I don't need to organise a time to see him or anyone that has crossed over. They are available, always. Just by thinking of them, I feel their love and their presence in my life. They may have left physically, but certainly not energetically or spiritually.

My Portals

Grief has gifted me the experience of the power of ***soul connection*** and how to connect with people who I miss, despite which plane, country or town they are residing on. This connection has brought a lightness and a feeling that we never truly lose anyone … well, not their soul or essence anyway.

✧

――――――― Thank you pain. Thank you, gifts. ―――――――

✧

Pain as a Portal

PORTAL PAINTINGS

☐ Grief makes me feel vulnerable. So does being naked. So, to invoke my body's remembrance of vulnerability, I painted naked, except for my friend's branded socks.

To start the painting 'grief', I closed my eyes to see my friend's gorgeous smiling face. Creating cracks in this piece was an obvious way to start, for reasons previously stated. I decided to burn the cracks in the wood, as I recall when he first passed, having a burning sensation in my heart where it ached. These cracks reminded me of lightning and how just like cracks and lightning, no two people's grief looks the same. It shatters and breaks open the surface, metaphorically, in an unpredictable way. I was also reminded that the night of my friend's passing, there was hours of thunder, lightning and a tornado that tore through our town, much like the tearing sensation of my heart. As I looked at the cracks, I was reminded of Kintsugi, the Japanese art of repairing broken ceramics by mending the pieces with urushi, gold lacquer. As a philosophy, this is an act of treating the breakage and repair as part of the history of an object, rather than something to disguise. I find this is a beautiful analogy for how we can look at ourselves and our wounds.

As I continued painting, my chest tightened, and tears fell. I wanted it to be over so I could start painting the other side. Steadying my breath, I was devoted to feeling what was presenting itself and slowly the intense sensations subsided.

Painting 'soul connection' was initially difficult. I was too in my head and the self-judgment of doing it justice. I would close my eyes and picture my friend's smile, laugh and energy, which dissipated the judgments. Such a gift cannot be explained or painted, to convey it purely. It must be felt. So, I decided to just have fun and paint as if we were together at a doof, and once finished we were going to leave it in a forest somewhere for fairies to cut up and build a house out of. Just like letting go of his body, I painted as if I had to let go of this wood at some point, yet keeping the connection to it.

'grief'
as a portal to
'soul connection'

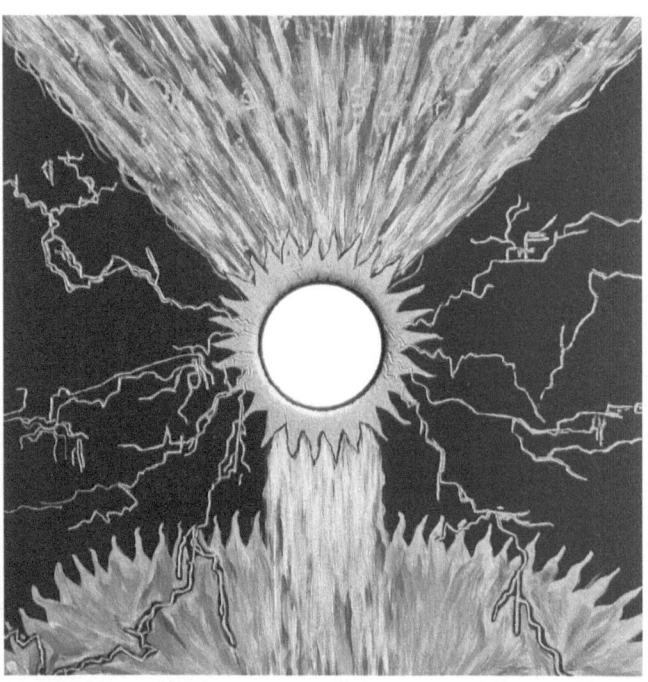

misunderstood as a *portal to* liberation

PHASE 1

Circa 5 years old

I started to feel ***misunderstood***, by my parents, sister and friends. I don't recall any specific event, just that I often felt like my intentions, essence, words, actions and entire being was being misunderstood.

PHASE 2

This feeling rattles my mind and makes my heart ache. It often invokes feelings of loneliness, aloneness, sadness, unworthiness, confusion, frustration and fury too. These feelings make me want to hide and to not show myself at all.

Pain as a Portal

PHASE 3

28+ years

I feel like I have been in this chrysalis for as long as I can remember, as I am met by these feelings regularly. It has gone from just family and friends, to feeling misunderstood by strangers, the world as a collective and the most painful, misunderstanding myself. I often feel frustrated or guilty if I misunderstand others, too.

My yearning to understand *why* this may be so, has led me down countless paths of curious inquiry. ☐ This consisted of ongoing observation of humans, paired with learning about human behaviour, psychology, philosophy and mysticism.

What it all seems to come back to is perception, the ability to see, hear, or become aware of something through the senses. This awareness however is also based upon a person's experiences, personality, belief systems and much more.

•

☐ While contemplating the concept of perception, I imagine a group of people standing in front of a flower that has just sprung up from the earth, that has never been identified before. Some of the people see beauty, some see ugliness, some find its scent delicious, while others hold their noses.

At the core, then, is truth. What is the truth of what that flower is? Are some people right and some wrong? Or is all of the above true? Or none of the above true? What is the truth? Who am I? What is existence? As you can see, a simple misunderstanding of my character launches me into existential inquiry, a spiral of wonder and sometimes a throbbing headache.

☐ By introducing intentional creative expression, in the form of countless discussions with friends, therapy, dance, reading books, art making, meditation, swimming, play, late night bubble baths and having picnics with nature, I have gathered some treasures that ease the pressure of this pain.

Some include:

- Acceptance that I will be understood by some, but not all.
- When I act with authentic and loving intentions, the less I care about feeling understood.
- That for me, feeling understood is to feel accurately perceived and peacefully acknowledged, not necessarily agreed with.
- The more I think I know about humans, the world, and myself, the more I realise how little I truly know. Sometimes residing in the not knowing or knowing nothing, is quite peaceful.
- If I take myself or life too seriously, the more it hurts. By reminding myself that all is well, or that all is as it should be, I feel grounded and in flow with the grace of life's intelligence.

•

As these realisations settled gradually in my being over some years, an unfamiliar energy started to grow within. During this time, interestingly, the world was experiencing a pandemic. My sense of freedom felt constricted, frustrated and furious by the government's rules and opinions. This sparked feeling overwhelming amounts of isolation, confusion and fear in my body.

☐ One of my favourite practices to do when I feel like I am being affected by things that are out of my control, is conceptual mirrorwork. This involves looking at what I am placing as an experience produced externally from the world—which is *out* of my control—as a mirror, to indicate how I may be creating the same experience internally—which is *in* my control. I questioned if there is anything I am doing to myself that makes me feel constricted, isolated, confused, frustrated and so on, and to be honest, there were many things I did to make myself feel like this. One area of life that called my attention that ignited *all* of these feelings, however, was being vegan.

☐ I had lengthy conversations about this with my partner, meditated, painted, danced, cried and sat in quiet contemplation of this subject. I felt very torn between my morals and what my body was telling me by its feelings. It became very apparent that the label of being vegan and sticking to all the rules around veganism, felt more detrimental to me than what I had ever realised. What I really wanted was to eat what I wanted, which was mostly vegan anyway, with occasional meat, cheese, chocolate and whatever delicious morsel was on the menu when out at a restaurant. After all, tasting flavours and textures brings me great joy, and life is all about experiencing the pleasures along with the pains.

It wasn't veganism that made me feel constricted, it was the label. Once I labelled that *I am* vegan, I felt like I had to identify and follow this label all of the time. I decided to free myself from it and from constricting and restricting myself from joy.

Following this, a feeling of freedom and liberation swelled within. I started to play with freeing myself from all the labels, one by one, to see how it felt. I discovered that they each felt like more of a hindrance than an aid. The only label that feels liberating, is to be 'April'. To be April entails the essence of all my everchanging parts, feelings, dreams, roles, the past, present and future.

•

This feeling of liberation rose and fell intermittently, as my frustration grew increasingly, not only by labels, but by words and language. The English language does not have the perfect words to describe most of what I want to express, about love, pain, life, experiences, feelings and concepts. So many words in society aren't used accurately, or they are overused, to the point of their meaning being diluted or changed. I can struggle to find the words or to articulate what I know or feel fully.

☐ I expressed this frustration creatively by dancing, painting, smiling, spending time with a dictionary and by sitting in silence. This combination calms me and brings me peace. This is what I love so much about creative expression. The combination of words, shapes, colours, movements and sounds is as close to truth as I can get.

This ignited memories about the time walking the Camino de Santiago, where speech was not required to connect or the many times that I have spent dancing and laughing with people who cannot speak. These memories are gifts that serve as loving reminders, that I do not need the perfect words to connect with people. Actually, sometimes the connection is much stronger without the conversations. I imagine a smile, frown or hug, the gift of homemade jam, the act of fixing my dripping tap or the energy of space being held for me in loving silence while I weep. These connections are liberating.

Pain as a Portal

PHASE 4

Writing this book has initiated me deeply into all of the above sensations. It has been a gift to me. I feel seen, heard and understood by my *self*, more than ever before.

I have discovered that when I feel misunderstood, I more-so feel fragmented or separate from my true self or others. I often need to remind myself that this is only my mind's perception, not my innate truth. Actually, the fact of my and our connection, oneness and wholeness is completely mind-blowing. When I give information time to settle in my brain, I soon start to feel it in my body. With time, it becomes knowing within my being, rather than my mind. This knowing alchemised my discomfort with the term healing along with every single other pain I have felt. Life in its totality is far beyond being able to be understood and therefore so am I.

Life is a mystery.
I am a mystery.

This changed the feeling of being misunderstood from being heavy and unpleasant into to a light pleasantness.

Understanding has led to self-compassion, letting go of having to know *all* the time and beaming **liberation**. I feel ready and excited to emerge and fly out into the world to show my many colours. The fear of being misunderstood visits, but not for long, as when I quiet the mind, and focus on my heart, all is well.

Realising my appreciation of the written word has also been a gift. Words connect me to so many people. I yearn to feel connected, much more than I yearn to feel understood. Without words, this book and my message would not be tangible. Sometimes, more words will be required, less words or different words, but

My Portals

eventually I am met with the many gifts of connection, wonder, understanding, questions and answers. When I feel liberated, the desire to feel understood or to explain myself subsides, which is a relief.

It also feels liberating to know that fellow humans cannot take any of my gifts from me, for they are found within myself and are always accessible.

As I write this, I am having trouble sitting still. My body wants to leap, spin and dance!

•

Let's end with a word that I came across in my studies: *oubaitori* – which means: (noun): the Japanese philosophy that people, like flowers, bloom in their own time and in their individual ways.

Now *that*, is the type of word that makes my soul smile.

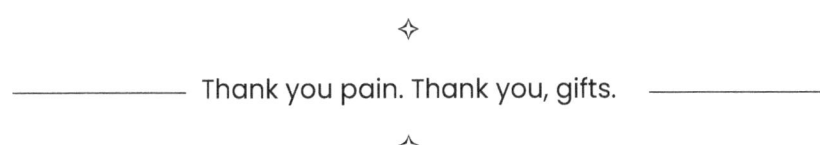
———— Thank you pain. Thank you, gifts. ————

PORTAL PAINTINGS

☐ As I stared at the black background of *'misunderstood'*, I contemplated how the dark blackness can be so misunderstood. The mind can create wild scenarios in an attempt to make sense of what it is perceiving. Putting colours down to symbolise perception further assisted to ease the pain of feeling misunderstood. It made it feel beautiful to see the many possibilities of perceptions. It made it even less about me and more about the mystery behind being perceived. While the pain of feeling misunderstood has morphed into feeling liberated, I feel like there is much more to explore in regard to the concept of being perceived and how all perceptions play a part in creating the spectrum of truth.

By painting *'liberation'* and spending time in communion with the feeling of liberation, it became apparent that this feeling had been dormant within me. Now that it has emerged, it is a warrior who is determined, courageous and excited to explore the human experience from a liberated perspective. It feels like the fire in my belly is blazing, yet there is a magical essence about it. It feels in equal balance of feminine and masculine in its power, and reminds me to be as weird, loving, and radical as possible.

❀

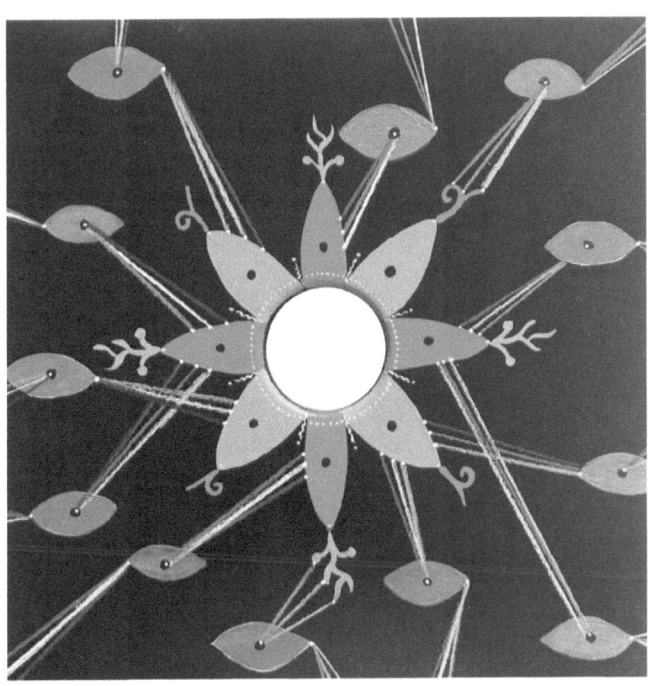

'misunderstood'
as a portal to
'liberation'

questions as a *portal to* knowing

PHASE 1

For as long as I can remember, I have asked many questions around the existence of humans on Earth.

> Who am I?
> Why am I here?
> What is the purpose of humans?
> What is my purpose?
> What is the purpose of everything?
> What else is out there?
> Why this body?
> And quite often, what the f***?

Pain as a Portal

PHASE 2

Amidst these **questions**, I have felt purposeless, frustrated, dismayed, confused, irritable, bored, empty, lonely, misunderstood.

PHASE 3

32 years and counting ...

Being human hurts. It's also rather beautiful and incredible. Oh, the sweet dualities!

☐ My yearning for answers to my questions led me to explore, in no particular order: non-fiction books, Sandplay Therapy, Art Therapy, hypnotism, past life regressions, tarot, psychic readings, personality tests, psychology, poetry, astrology, the gene keys, mediumship, various types of jobs, psychedelic drugs, art making, music, sex, ecstatic dance, reiki, moving towns, moving countries, meditation and much more.

All of these have been amazing tools to understand a vast variety of concepts. They have each been a gift and sustenance for my journey. Most of these gave the answers to my questions, which surprisingly, my body and mind felt frustrated by. I realised that I didn't want to be told the answers. I wanted to remember them and know them in my heart, blood and bones.

•

After spending most of my life looking for the answers outside of myself, I could finally apply I.C.E. ☐ I asked my pain questions. I danced with them, painted them, talked about them and meditated on them. While language isn't my preferred form of expression, some language provides incredible insight. One day, as I was in deep contemplation of *Who am I? What am I?* The words *I am a human being* presented themselves ever so slowly, separating each word to give them space to stand individually.

> I. Am. A. Human. Being.
> I am being.
> I am in a state of being.
> How do I feel when I am simply being? Oh my, I am home!
> And when I am home, I feel like I have purpose. I feel limitless!
> So, my purpose is to *be*?

Initially this seemed a bit underrated and easy, until I gave it more space to settle. As I trialled it, I realised that simply being is actually the hardest thing about being human. There's so much distraction, confusion and longing that pulls me either into the past or the future. I am not a Human Was or Human Going to Be. Those places are where a lot of my pain lives. Well, I'll *be*.

This train of thought continued …

> When I am a human feeling, I am my feelings.
> When I am a human thinking, I am my thoughts.
> When I am a human doing, I am those tasks.

Whatever I place my attention on, my mind clings to this as Who I am in totality. Who I AM, is all of those parts and none of those parts simultaneously. Every moment, every sensation, every feeling passes. So, my am-ness is always in motion. I am energy in motion, in form, in a moment of time. I am limitless. How exhilarating!

•

In my early 30s, when the world experienced the COVID-19 pandemic, I felt like I was living a different reality to most. The majority of people were acting in ways that felt foreign to me. Despite connecting with people who had a similar perception of what was happening in the world, I found it incredibly difficult to just be me. Being me felt lonely and as though I could have been under attack at any time for not following the majority. This reminded my body of the many times throughout my life that I had felt this.

My spirit was slowly descending into what felt like the deep, darkest part of the ocean. I had experienced this descent before, so it didn't scare me, but it was uncomfortable.

☐ When the social heat of this worldwide movement had reduced, I went to a music festival, as this usually enlivens my spirit. I felt intense emotional agony. Being around people and the music made my body buzz, and I was on the edge of panic for days. I tried taking chemically created ecstasy to shift my state, which only made me feel more vulnerable. I spent most of my time hiding in my van with my boyfriend.

The week after this, I attended a Women's Gathering with a few friends, consisting of lots of enriching workshops and conversations. I was still feeling quite sensitive, so when the large dance event was about to start, I retreated, to walk back to my van.

My Portals

I'm not sure what made me turn around, but I did and oh my, I am glad I did. The moon was rising over the dancehall, beaming with vibrancy, owning its place in the sky. I stared longingly into her glow as she enticed me to dance.

✶ This was my first experience of the ecstatic dance practice called Dancing Freedom. There was no choreography, only an invitation to move your body in whatever way it desired. I was used to bobbing along to the beat at music festivals so when I saw other people moving their bodies in all ways imaginable, I felt incredibly vulnerable. I started with slow movement until courage rose within me. My body moved in ways that my brain was very surprised by. At the end of the dance, I fell to the floor sobbing in amazement. This was the first time that I could remember ever feeling completely free, liberated and full of ecstasy *in* my body, solely created by my own body. No drugs. No alcohol. No energetic transfer from another. I felt at home in my body and alive! During this dance, my mind ceased seeking meaning and I could just be.

•

The Dancing Freedom session was one of those experiences that my mind, body and soul craved, so I took training to understand the practice at an intellectual and an embodied level, not only for myself but to then be certified to facilitate these dances for my community. This was medicine.

The Dancing Freedom practice promotes being in a devoted right relationship with ourselves, each other and nature, specifically working in harmony with the elements, earth, water, fire, air and ether. This connection and devotion is woven into all parts of the

Pain as a Portal

dance, from the altar to the music choices, to how each leader dances with life.

At this point in time, the concept of pain as a portal was already bouncing around in my mind and I had started playing with it in my daily life and in my work. This training, however, was filled with an unlimited supply of validation alongside further experiences that serenaded my intellectual knowledge of this concept, my cells, blood, nervous system and bones. As I danced with the elements to get to know them better, I also danced with the pains of my past and present, giving them movement and shape. I screamed. I cried. I stood still amongst the chaos of the dance, to feel them simmer in my body.

☐ One theme of the dance was trance. We were all blindfolded and the music was solely the electronic genre of trance. This assisted me to enter into a trance state of consciousness very quickly.

✦ I envisioned dropping down through all of the most unpleasant dense emotions. Like in an elevator, slowly arriving at each level to feel each individual uncomfortable emotion intensely. I met the likes of grief, fear, anger, shame and guilt, until finally landing at the bottom, in a pit of fire, surrounded by darkness. This pit encompassed all that was dark—my shadow, my evil. I felt scared and surprisingly empowered. I knew that as I had now met these aspects face-to-face, that they no longer held fearful power over me and that I was able to transcend them. My body started moving like a snake, shedding its skin, revealing my new scales of awareness and trust.

I was then transported upwards, to a space of infinite bright light. It was so bright that my cells felt like they were screaming. As I adjusted, I knew I was in the place I call home. The sensations of peace, tranquillity, playfulness and love was breathtaking. Just as I was starting to get comfortable, I was transported to a forest where I was told by various beings that one of my missions on earth was to meet all beings in their pain and to *be you* until they transcend their pain. Despite their message being relayed, this was not new information, my soul *remembered* it. I suddenly remembered my soul choosing that this time on earth was to experience every feeling that a human could experience. It was not only to experience the full spectrum of humanness, but to be able to relate and connect to all beings which is the foundation of relationship. I had the realisation and remembrance that while our experiences are all different, our pain or pleasure in response to the experience is where our oneness resides. This is why your pain hurts me. Whichever feeling you are experiencing; it punches the place in me where I have felt that too and I am able to empathise.

To be me is to express myself, as all of my aspects, in any given moment. The sticky, the uncomfortable, the sad, the angry, the playful, the ecstatic, the peaceful. To know myself, is to know you.✦

The music stopped and my awareness was back in my body, back in the room. My body entered into a brief state of shock, followed by an excited desire to retreat back to my room to integrate.

•

For the next eight months and counting, I continued to revel intermittently in joy, courage, inquisitiveness, empowerment, contentedness, playfulness and inspiration. All of these feelings assisted me to embark onwards, to dance the dance of life. I now know that when I crave answers, this is a reminder to be present. When I am present, I am free from the pain that my mind creates, and I feel all that I am. Each and every time it is a homecoming.

Pain as a Portal

Remembering my decision to experience it all initiated a new ability to respond to myself, aka self-responsibility, which released all judgement about previous experiences and a new level of understanding and gratitude for them. My experiences started to feel like they were happening *for* me, rather than *to* me.

•

☐ Something special that has soothed all of my pains, but especially this one, has been to spend time with people who feel like home. There is only a small handful of people that feel like this. To be myself without holding back, is the scariest form of intentional creative expression that I have tried. But these people make it easy. Sometimes I tell them my pain, but simply being in their presence calms me and reminds me just how lucky I am to be on Earth. They listen, hold me, make me laugh and I feel loved, just as I am. ✷ They have been some of my most treasured gifts along the way. They make the questions fade and not matter.

•

☐ One of my other favourite ways to partake in intentional creative expression is to sit and spend time with my soul. The quickest way to get there, I find, is to close my eyes. As my eyelids drop and with every breath out, I fall deeper into the darkness, where the most potent silence resides. I ask what it is that my pain wants me to know. As I surrender to fall deeper and deeper into this space, I feel my pain, ego, and thoughts slowly dissipate. The silence has a lot to say. Sometimes I get answers, but every single time without fail, I feel more peaceful, appreciative and more at one with all of existence, than I did beforehand. The stars, blades of grass, wind, water and earth feel like friends. The Indigenous Peoples of my land call this *dadirri* which means deep listening. Others call it meditation or communion with source. I feel my body vibrate, in rhythm with the universe, in the now. What a beautiful place to be. This is knowing.

PHASE 4

I have not yet emerged from this chrysalis. I have been gifted with glimpses into **knowing** the truth of my questions time and time again but underneath this brief relief, are more questions, wonder and occasional doubt.

Most of what aches, is directly attributed to the ego, what it creates within me and others. I like to imagine that as our humanity evolves and we enter into our collective chrysalis, all but the soul dissolves and we emerge with a consciousness that only radiates knowing, love, understanding, gratitude and oneness.

As I continue to apply I.C.E and cultivate patience and self-compassion within, I am reminded not to rush or force this process. My wings of knowing will be spectacular, in full flight, in due course, but alas I must have more to accept, learn, unlearn, morph and discover.

✧

Thank you pain. Thank you, gifts.

✧

Pain as a Portal

PORTAL PAINTINGS

☐ The more I experience the pleasures of being a human, the less questions I seek answers to. I waited to paint *'questions'* until a day that I felt lost and unsure. The day visited in January 2024. Nothing was particularly painful about the day. The sun was glorious yet wonder took hold of my mind. I decided to turn to the paints and let my mind off the hook, to try make sense of its stirring thoughts. I closed my eyes, and my hands felt like reaching to the sky. I started to paint this and very quickly I felt peace surround me in an embrace. This embrace felt like the chrysalis. Warm and reassuring, that I am exactly where I am supposed to be, and everything is as it should be. This is what inspired the painting *'knowing'*.

❁

'questions'
as a portal to
'knowing'

pleasure
as a portal to
!!!

PHASE 1

Birth.

PHASE 2

I have been blessed in this lifetime, to be able to feel ***pleasure***, to varying degrees, no matter what challenges I am experiencing. Feeling the pleasurable feelings—the depths, shapes, corners, edges, colours and frequencies is intoxicating.

Pain as a Portal

PHASE 3

Minutes, hours, days ...

During my early 20s I certainly lost touch with just how much pleasure was available to me, so much so that in my late 20s I had to re-learn how to truly experience pleasure. It became apparent that not long after experiencing a pleasurable emotion, joy, happiness, bliss, love, calm, ecstasy or orgasm, I would quickly experience guilt for feeling these when there was so much pain in the world, or the busyness of life overrode it, and it dissipated instantly into the past.

Using The PAIN Process to re-learn how to experience pleasure to its fullest, has been a tender path to tread. Initially, I had to simultaneously sink into the pain of guilt or stress to discover their messages or gifts. The message was resoundingly repetitive. *You deserve joy. Life is about balance. How can you empower people if you are stuck in the pain or the shadow of life? Life will serve you yours. Life can be joyous, fun, and full of play. Life is limitless.* You get the picture. Once I accepted and decided to say yes to pleasure and applied I.C.E to the pleasure (imagine me here winking, with a cheeky grin), pleasure started to last longer and longer and eventually was readily available in every moment, simultaneously to pain. Sure, it was always available, but now I could access, embrace, and wade in it.

✷ I find pleasure in silence, kindness, smiles, love, rainbows, lovemaking, dancing, poetry, painting, the night sky, the day sky, nature, friends, family, animals, colours, music, hugs, kisses, laughter, food, scents, moments of purity and the elements in all of their states. I find it in witnessing humans grow and expressing themselves with honesty, vulnerability and courage, until their pure essence of light peaks through their cracks. I can find it in all that exists, really, if I put on my spectacles that allow me to see the light of what I am looking at.

☐ My favourite intentional forms of creative expression of pleasure are to smile, laugh, hug, cry, walk, swim, dance, skip, paint, write, speak, love, and meditate, on repeat.

PHASE 4

Whenever I apply I.C.E to a pleasurable sensation or feeling, I very quickly burst out of the chrysalis of that feeling and into a more intense sensation of the original pleasure, embellished with a sprinkle of other pleasures, which are all encompassed by an orb of light. It feels like gratitude explodes out of my heart uncontrollably and reverberates far beyond my being, as if it is reaching all corners of the universe. I feel at one with it all and myself at my truest essence. There aren't adequate words to describe the gift of where I go or how I feel through this portal, so stars and exclamation marks will suffice *!!!*

I am still learning, to not *hold on* too tightly to these feelings—to let them go, gracefully—when it is their natural time to dissipate into my body and the universe. When I do, I am always lovingly reminded that this is the space in between, where more experience can grow.

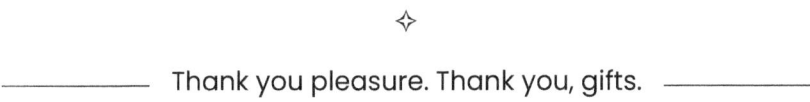

———— Thank you pleasure. Thank you, gifts. ————

Pain as a Portal

PORTAL PAINTINGS

☐ My intention was to have as much fun as I could while painting *'pleasure'* & *'*!!!*'*. I put on dance music, ate chocolate, made a huge mess and danced with the colours. My inner child pleaded me to stick on rhinestone gems, as she has always loved stickers. Child April and Adult April had a ball! It took hours to finish in between the dancing, spinning, swinging on the swing, making snacks, playing with my dog, singing and reminiscing about all the pleasure that my being recalls.

❋

'pleasure'
as a portal to
'*!!!*'

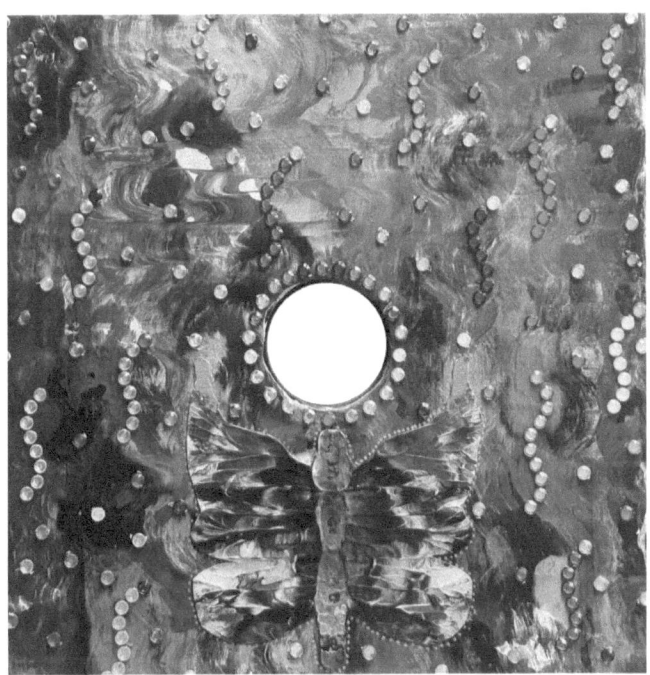

all of my pleasure and pain as a *portal to* this book

PHASE 1

My conception.

PHASE 2

Every experience, every feeling of **pleasure & pain** felt, absorbed and morphed, to date.

Pain as a Portal

PHASE 3

2 years

I entered this chrysalis in early 2022, the day in the pine forest, pleading for answers. For the next six months, occasional realisations, correlations, analogies, concepts and understandings formed in my mind.

Later that year, I started having repeated experiences of my entire body feeling like it was filled with buzzing bees and then suddenly, they would all fly to their Queen, who resided in the centre of my forehead. This buzz was excruciatingly painful. I'd then get streams of full sentences which all seemed related to comparing the metamorphosis in butterflies to humans. They felt invasive. I have become well practiced in acknowledging feelings that rise in me, so I knew they wanted to be expressed creatively. ☐ Through some experimentation, the only way to make the pain stop, was to write the sentences down. The moment they were written, *poof* ... the pain would vanish. It was like all the bees had departed to go and find more nectar from fields of flowers, to bring back to me transformed into sentences. This would happen at the most unhelpful times, like in the shower, when I was with clients or friends, in the middle of the night, during sex and when in the supermarket. I couldn't stop and write them down in most of these scenarios. The buzzing pain would stay until I could though. Sentences were all around my house on Post-It notes, in journals, my phone, my laptop, serviettes and whatever that was close by, to release them from my mind. I had told a few friends, so with them I could often pause our conversation, write the thought down, laugh and return to the conversation with my full attention. This continued for approximately one month. Once I got the crux of the model of this process written, the buzzing ceased.

I started to wonder what I should do with this information. It was becoming more than just a conversation to have with people. ☐ I meditated. During this meditation, I went to an empty white glowing room and asked for the Queen Bee of this information to meet me. A glowing, colour changing portal instead presented itself, so I asked some questions:

> Is this just for me?
> *No.*
>
> Is this just for my clients?
> *No.*
>
> Do you want to be a book?
> *Yes.*
>
> Should I share my personal experiences?
> *Yes.*
>
> Do you want to be art?
> *Yes.*
>
> Dance?
> *Yes.*
>
> Is this something that continually transforms?
> *Yes.*

The portal then disappeared. I opened my eyes. I was feeling increasingly nauseous at the thought of all of this, until I began to feel excited, intrigued, inspired and courageous.

Pain as a Portal

So, here we are! This book and whatever else this information morphs into, is the tribute to pain, pleasure, Intentional Creative Expression and our Mettāmorphosis.

•

I have a very full life. Most of my days are intentionally designated in my calendar, to all areas of my life that I want to connect with. The majority of my time is devoted to being with the people who use my therapeutic services. Those meetings contain so much magic. ✳ I get to journey the path of self-inquiry with the most incredible humans. It was time to start collating the sentences though. I found it very difficult to immerse myself in this process for an hour here or there, as part of my awareness was tied up into time and where I was required next. I wanted to sink into the depths of the experience of it and be completely present. I didn't want to rearrange my calendar, as when I commit my time to something, especially people who are ready to shift their pain, it's important to me to honour that commitment.

☐ For the past few years, I have trialled not working during the school holidays, to devote my attention to myself. A few holidays passed and I'd get small amounts of this book done, but I would easily get pulled in different directions, by adventures in nature, spending time with loved ones, domestic tasks or making an aquarium out of Lego. Then before I knew it, the holidays were over. I would feel incredibly irritated with myself and with the Universe for taking my attention elsewhere. After crying or stomping, I would come back to a peaceful place of acceptance, as I believe everything happens for a reason, whether I am privy to that reason or not.

My Portals

•

☐ In the July 2023 holidays however, I wrote and painted for ten days straight, for up to ten hours a day. I was blessed with a sinus infection during this time. I chuckled, as for a mere moment in time, I felt ever so slightly annoyed, before being quickly carried away into a state of wonder. What if, all of these little germs got together with food and drinks, to plan a way to keep me home, without being *too* unwell, so I could stay emersed and focused? ✸ I typically believe the Universe looks after me, so this was no exception, despite the delivery of that support.

A few days in, I saw that Sigur Rós had released a new album, *Átta*. The sounds and frequencies of each track felt like they were designed *for me*, for *this process*. Of course they were not, but yet again I was gifted with the sensation of support. ✸ When I played this music, it felt like all the silky threads of my existence, that were spread all over the universe, were lovingly gathered by these frequencies and delivered back to my centre. I felt centred, as all of me was humming with presence, at the surface of my heart. It felt heavy, causing my heart to throb with aliveness, light and exhilaration. I tried putting on other music, but my spirit always pulled me back to this album. The crackle of the fire weaved in symbiotic partnership with each song reverberating around me, on repeat. As my physical unwellness passed, I started to get distracted by other things, but by putting on this album, I felt myself anchored into myself and devoted to this process once again.

Átta is Icelandic for eight. Symbolising the band's eighth studio album. I gleam as I contemplate the infinite shape of 8 and how the music makes me feel like I am floating through infinite peace and possibility. Also, that eight is my life path number in numerology, another synchronistic message and wink of support from the infinite.

✷ My beautiful dog laid beside me the entire time. Hours would pass and I would be broken out of the spell of creative flow by him having a burst of energy to play, which was always exactly when I needed a break.

It wasn't until I finished writing the chapters of my personal portals that I realised there were nine. This number held no conscious significance to me. I researched the meaning of the numerology of the number nine, which certainly gave me goosebumps.

The paintings were also now done. Seeing them all together created an absolute mixed bag of lollies of emotions within me. Relief and grief that it was finished, amazement, happiness, wonder of what was to come and a contentedness. I bought them a bunch of roses to thank them for everything they had done for me and blew them kisses.

•

I decided to spend time with the butterfly, in all its phases, to learn directly from my teacher. I purchased some Monarch caterpillars however nature had its way, and they were not able to be delivered. I was offered six chrysalides as an alternative, which I gratefully accepted. When they arrived at my doorstep in a typical package, it was quite absurd, imagining them going on a journey from a butterfly house, into a box, into multiple post offices, in the car with the postman and delivered at my door. When I opened the packaging, each individual chrysalis was wrapped in cotton wool. How apt. I opened them gently, with the most care I possibly could. They were attached to small earring hooks to then be hung in a small mesh cube provided, to make their new house. They were completely still. The outside surface of the chrysalis was cold and so smooth that it felt wet. I hung them in their new cube home and adorned the base of the cube with an altar, consisting of plant-life, water, crystals, and a figurine of me, so that they could feel the frequency of their home, was that of only love and gratitude for the gift that they were bringing me and this process.

✸ I found it incredibly difficult to carry on with life, as all I wanted to do, was lie by them, be with them, in stillness. I sobbed as I realised that the level of care and tenderness I offered them, was not the level of care and tenderness I usually offer myself. It was a mirror, that when I am in pain, my heart is aching, and I am evolving and that this is how I should treat my heart and my body. Did they know how vulnerable, fragile, and yet beautiful and strong they are in this state? As I softened into that question, I asked this to myself. Grief rose as I realised that the immediate answer was no. I lay next to them, mirroring them in their stillness and patience. There was nowhere else to be except in the mush of their transformation. I breathed, as gently as I could, into my body, softening all the edges and all of the resistance, as an offering to send my being and my grief, the tenderness that I am willing to offer to others. I started to feel my vulnerability, fragility and beauty come to the surface to meet me, comfort me and remind me that I am deserving of this tenderness, not only when in this state, but always. While I laid there in stillness, I felt at complete peace. I think back to the butterfly in the pine forest and realised it wasn't a messenger *from* source, it was direct communication *with* source. In this state, completely quiet within, I realised that it was time to give myself permission to slow down, to savour the gentle moments in between and to move at a graceful pace.

A few weeks passed. Each day their outer shell slowly changed colour from lime green, to black, to transparent, showing the colours and shapes of their wings. Whenever I walked past them, I would say hello and check on them. It was hard to go to work, as all I wanted to do was to be with them. The day finally came, where when I walked past, one of the butterflies had emerged. It hung onto its now empty chrysalis, while its wings hardened. It practiced moving its wings, legs and proboscis. Tears fell and my chest space ached, as I so badly wanted to witness their emerging. I heard a small crackling sound and looked up to see the next butterfly was emerging. It was breathtaking to witness. The amazement overwhelming. This made me want to spend my time with them even more. I was very lucky to see two of the six butterflies emerge.

Once they all became active in their little house, that meant it was time to release them. To honour the full cycle, I released them at the pine forest, where this all began. They climbed onto my finger and the moment they felt the air, off they flew! The first few flaps were a little wobbly, then they glided through the air with grace. Before I knew it, they were out of sight. My heart ached; tears fell. Letting them go came with pain. I had become quite attached to them and didn't want them to leave. This reminded me of the grief that I often feel, when emerging from my emotional chrysalis. The freedom and change can arrive with shock, wondering whether I want to crawl back into my dark chrysalis that I have come to know so well … But alas, we cannot, and after a little wobble, taking flight and breathing in the freedom is incredible.

A few weeks later, the six caterpillars I initially ordered arrived. My excitement was very childlike. I set up their little house and popped them in, along with plenty of milkweed to eat. For days on end, they munched and munched and munched away. They grew very quickly. My mum reminded me that when I was little, I used to call them pillar pillars, so this is how we continued to refer to them from then on. Suddenly, they all climbed to the top of their house and were still, for over a day. Worry, that I had done something wrong, set in. Thankfully, one of them started to visibly show convulsions and slowly released silk to create a pad. It used its hook-covered appendage, called a cremaster, to attach itself to this pad. It wriggled and twisted around, embedding its cremaster firmly in the silk. It hung in the shape of a J for a while. Its head produced a lime green, soft, skin-like texture, which soon enclosed the entire caterpillar. Its final moult popped out of the top and it sealed itself completely. It gradually became smooth, gold dots became visible, and its chrysalis set, a protective shell for it to morph into a butterfly. The other five caterpillars followed suit.

As the next few weeks passed, I loved having my morning cup of tea with them whilst playing Sigur Rós' album, reading them poetry and telling them my woes. Their chrysalis darkened, became transparent and this time I knew their emergence wasn't far away. When those moments came for them to emerge, it was like seeing it for the first time. The awe was magnified. Time and everything else in the world ceased to exist. The purity of the miracle of metamorphosis and of life, encapsulated me.

I pondered about how so often, when we can visibly see a transformation taking place in front of our eyes, we enter into a state of awe and amazement. Yet, we rarely do for transformations we do not witness tangibly. I want humanity to evolve into feeling this level of awe for the intrinsic transformations that take place within us. I want us to acknowledge our changes, growth and learnings and celebrate them.

The day came to release them into the wild. This time, I decided to release them in my backyard. The grief of letting them go rose, as they had become my friends, but gratitude for them soon

Pain as a Portal

overrode the sad sensations. Some stayed on a flower close by for a few minutes before flying into the sky, while others flew with the wind the moment they were out of their house. Again, seeing them take flight was breathtaking. I went inside to inspect their empty chrysalises. I tugged on them to get them off the roof of the enclosure. I was amazed at how hard I had to pull to get them off. Their silk created a web that spread all around the area, not just the hanging point. It was so soft and slightly sticky. Their empty chrysalis shells were fragile and crackly.

About ninety minutes later, I returned to the menial human task of heading outside to put the washing out. One of the butterflies flew past me! I knew it was one of them as I never see Monarch's in my yard. She flew and perched on the tree outside my kitchen window. Happiness rose in my body as I was excited to spend a little bit more time with her. I made a cup of coffee and sat on a stool near my kitchen window to watch her. I decided to put on Sigur Rós' album as it evokes such intense feelings within me. Much to my amazement, another one of the Monarch's flew by and landed on this tree. Then, another butterfly! Upon closer inspection it was the variety of butterfly that I first saw in the pine forest, the day I pleaded for help. Tears fell down my cheeks as I laughed in astonishment of what I was witnessing. I was now mere sentences away from finishing this book, and here we all were, together. The butterfly from where it all began, the butterfly who deepened my understanding of the process of metamorphosis, frequencies of Sigur Rós and me. It was beautiful. The monarch stayed in this position for many hours. It was nice to spend some unexpected extra time with her. I've never enjoyed washing up so much. Glancing up at her was such a gift!

Now, whenever I see a butterfly, my heart smiles in unison with my mouth. I wonder if every butterfly is the physical manifestation of a human who has just emerged from an emotional chrysalis.

My Portals

Oh, how wonderful if that were to be true. I close my eyes and send a telepathic, *I'm so happy for you*, to the soul out there that has just emerged and is taking flight with their newfound gifts. This thought brings me a lot of joy.

•

☐ Intentionally marking my body through therapeutic tattooing, has been an important part of my many processes. This one was no different. In October 2023, with the book mostly finished, minus this chapter and editing, I received my markings that symbolised all that 'mettāmorphosis' encompassed and my commitment to this process. A butterfly was placed on each arm, as if each served as a portal in, through my heart space and out the other side. We put on Sigur Rós and talked about life as we perceive it, along with spacious silences so I could focus on my intention and receiving this marking. Time started to suggest that the tattoos wouldn't be able to be finished, and I was asked to contemplate how I felt about this. After initial discomfort, it dawned on us that of course they couldn't be finished, as I hadn't emerged from the chrysalis of this experience yet, so of course this was perfect. So, we intentionally left the body of the butterflies to be finished for when the book had been finished and, or I felt ready. It was the first time that I have felt little to no pain or discomfort whilst receiving a tattoo. At one point, I felt like I had entered an altered state of pure bliss and was surrounded by butterflies. I then started to imagine many chrysalides hanging in the wild and wondered what albums of music each pupae liked to listen to whilst they were transforming.

Over the next few days, as these markings physically landed in my skin, there were periods of intense heat. Emotions and sensations started to flood my body. I practiced sitting, with eyes shut to feel

Pain as a Portal

everything my body was asking me to feel. The buzzing bees from the beginning of this entire process had returned, except this time, flying to these markings as though they were coming to inspect this new presence in their home. They suddenly disappeared. I had a wave of worry that they did not approve. Doubts started to enter my rational mind. I sat and felt these feelings, saying hello. The bees returned promptly. My arms were buzzing but simultaneously started to tickle, and then felt wet. I surrendered to this feeling, pleasant yet unpleasant, until I realised it felt like they were putting honey on the wounds. I felt so cared for and blessed. The buzzing gradually lessened over the following days, as my skin entered into the stage of itchiness, shedding and as new skin grew to close the wounds. Over the next two months, I felt this area of skin dancing, rearranging and preparing my cells to embody the intention of the markings. Despite the tattoo visually being wings, I very much felt like I was in chrysalis. My internal world felt busy. I continued to work away on this final chapter.

•

After this chapter was finished, I returned to receive the markings to close and finish the butterflies. Again, a very pleasurable experience physically and where my mind wandered into fantastical places in the ether. When they were finished, my tattoo therapist closed the space in ceremony, by drumming and singing. When the space was closed, I had a rush of energy wash over me, closely followed by the emotions of grief. I closed my eyes to listen deeply to what this grief had to say. I could see many faces, which I did not cognitively recognise, yet I had a felt sense that these faces were those of my ancestors, from both my paternal and maternal line. Some held expressions of joy and celebration, while others were resentful and disapproving. Holding onto pain has been 'the way' for many generations within my family, so I validated their feelings and assured them that this 'way' will serve us all. The intensity of their projected emotion lessened, and their faces faded. I opened my eyes to see my tattoo therapist, holding his presence sturdy yet gently, and I released a breath of relief.

The sensation of being in a subtle trance, stayed present for over a week. A sense of *I'm ready* and bravery filled my body. The first day that my skin had finished closing the wounds, synchronised with the day to release the butterflies. The closure physically, emotionally, intellectually and metaphorically was perfect, as nature always is.

Not long afterwards, symptoms of burnout and a return of a sinus infection presented themselves. These symptoms stayed for over seven months, as I slowly tried to decode their many messages and to implement the changes in my lifestyle that they were seeking. Some of the major messages were around restoration, living in rhythm with the rhythmic cycle of female hormones and menstruation, spending more time on serving my own needs rather than others and the importance of integration. I took time off work to allow my body time and space to catch its breath. I spent a week in my house, mostly simply lying on my back in front of the fire, or in the bath, in complete stillness, as many sensations buzzed and settled in my body. Many painful memories came to my mind with these sensations. I gave each of them as much time as they needed to rise and dissolve. I do wonder whether because the symbols of phase 4 were embedded into my body, that maybe my body was trying to fast-track all of my pains into their final phase. I hugged my body, reminding it of the importance of all the phases of mettāmorphosis and that there was no race to the final phase. After doing this daily, along with making a few other changes to my daily life, my symptoms eased significantly.

Pain as a Portal

PHASE 4

These are the final words written before sending this manuscript to the editor.

It is amazing to reflect, that at the time of each of my experiences, my mind was completely consumed and affected by them. Moving through these experiences and their portals has created a gentle hum within me, where I can recollect their existence, however they each feel like a mere drop in the ocean of my consciousness. For me, intentional creative expression is purely a way to connect to source within us and for source to express itself through us, in its many ways. By closing the chapters of all the stories told, they no longer feel required to be told again, to myself or others. My body feels lighter, spacious, and open for more experiences to land.

During the process of writing this book, I felt like a three-course meal, with an entree of vulnerability, a main of excitement, a side plate of relief, a beverage of curiosity, and purposefulness as dessert. **This book** serves as cutlery, to help me devour all that is in front of me, and all that is to come.

✧

_____ Thank you pain. Thank you pleasure. _____
Thank you, gifts.

✧

An honouring

Below is a dedicated container, to lovingly hold space for all the pains, pleasures and gifts that:

- I have not shared
- Feel tender and fresh, wanting to be just for me, to revel in for at least for the moment
- I am yet to meet.

Unwavering Gratitude

Words cannot express the gratitude and love that I feel in my body, on a regular basis. My hope is that every being that I have co-lived with on this planet *feels* it without doubt. Each of you have been *gifts* in my life.

To my dreamboat, you know me intrinsically on every level and you not only accept me, but you love me for who I am. That is the ultimate gift of my lifetime. Your joy, authenticity, patience, forgiveness and support are appreciated beyond measure. *You* are a daily gift, not only to me, but to Mo, our community and this planet. *Thank you.*

To my friends and family, these labels do not come even close to accurately defining the beauty of our relationships. Each of you bring your own individual magic to my life. You are all so precious to me. *Thank you.*

To Morris, you are my soulmate in dog form and a daily source of joy and love. *Thank you.*

To my counsellor, you have been such a sturdy, reliable, wise and loving pillar of support and guidance. This, along with saying yes to reading and doing the first edits of this book with tenderness, honesty and care, is so appreciated. *Thank you.*

To the practitioners who have supported me through their craft such as tattoo, energy consultancy, reiki, kinesiology, astrology, meditation, massage, acupuncture and tarot. *Thank you.*

To the people who share their pains with me, your trust, openness, vulnerability and courage is treasured. To the parents and carers who trust me to spend time with their children to explore and care for their pains. *Thank you.*

To all the people who I do not personally know, yet I feel like I know, as you have influenced and inspired me through your books, music, art and words of wisdom. *Thank you.*

To the infinite beauty and treasures that life on earth provides; the sun, air, earth, water, fire, soil, food, mushrooms, flowers, animals, rainbows, music, colour, textures, patterns, scents, and tastes, to name but a mere few. *Thank you.*

To my ancestors who walked before me and continue to walk with me, my benevolent guides and allies. *Thank you.*

To the full spectrum of experiences and emotions that life as a human offers me every day. *Thank you.*

To my teachers the egg, caterpillar, pupae and butterfly and all of your wise teachings and guidance. *Thank you.*

To Natasha and the team at The Kind Press, for saying yes to publishing this book and your loving-kindness every step along the way of the publication process. *Thank you.*

To all the people who walked alongside me and provided ongoing encouragement whilst writing 'the book'. *Thank you.*

To **you**—the reader, for your openness to explore and connect with me through these pages. *Thank you.*

To all that is. *Thank you.*

This body of work is a co-creation with all that I have mentioned above. Your impact on my life has played a part in bringing this together. How spectacular.

Closing Note

I am April Simone – which in Latin means, *to open, to listen.*

My name has been my lighthouse, guiding me home. It has been my greatest teacher, in that as long as I am closed, I will simmer in pain. When I open and listen to all that is, I am adorned with an abundance of gifts.

For as long as I breathe, I know that the journey of mettāmorphosis continues. Perhaps, it continues beyond that breath too. What a delightful prospect.

I am left wondering though, what if *we* are one of the Universe's intentional creative expressions and all gifts to provide sustenance to the chrysalis of existence, of all that is? Imagine the gift yet to emerge...

I send you love, for your journey,

April

Tribute To Works Of Art

I have steadfast gratitude and respect for each of the following people and the works of art that they share, as they have all been incredibly impactful and inspiring gifts to my life.

Authors & Texts

Asia Suler - Mirrors in the Earth
Barbara Marciniak - Bringers of the Dawn
Bessel Van Der Kolk - The Body Keeps The Score
Brené Brown - Atlas of The Heart, Daring Greatly
Bruce Lipton - The Biology of Belief
Carl Jung - Various
Caroline Myss - Anatomy of the Spirit
Clarissa Pinkola Estes - Women Who Run With The Wolves
Dalai Lama - The Art of Happiness
David Hawkins - Various
Donald Klsched - Trauma and the Soul
Helen Schucman - A Course in Miracles
Eckhart Tolle - The Power of the Now, A New Earth
Gabor Mate - The Myth of Normal
James Redfield - The Celestine Prophecy
Joe Dispenza - Becoming Supernatural
Kelly McGonigal - The Joy of Movement
Laozi - Tao Te Ching
Louise Hay - You Can Heal Your Life
Paulo Coelho - The Alchemist
Rhonda Byrne - The Magic
Robert Lee Potter - Letters from 500
Richard Bach - Illusions & Jonathon Livingston Seagull
Richard Rudd - The Gene Keys

Sally Morgan - The World Encyclopedia of Butterflies & Moths
Sara Blondin - Heart Minded
Sy Montgomery - The Soul of an Octopus
Terry Pratchett - Various
The Kybalion Hermetic Philosophy
Thomas Moore - Dark Nights of the Soul
Toko-pa Turner – Belonging, Remembering Ourselves Home
Walter Russel - The Universal One
Wayne Dyer - The Power of Intention
Zach Bush – Various

Artists & Art

Andy Goldsworthy • Anna Seed • Aphra Natley • Ben Lopez • Betsy Walton • Bunnie Reiss • Deedee Cheriel • Del Kathryn Barton • Delta Venus • Emma Black • Felix Saturn • Gabriela Rhinier • Hannah Yata • Hilma af Klint • James R. Eads • Jennifer Latour • Josephine Klerks • Lucy Pierce • Mark Nara • Marina Gonzalezeme • Mother Earth • Thomas Cruz Marten • Olive Jade • Paula Duro • Raine Alexandra • Rithika Merchant • Rose Unfolding • Rosetta Santucci • Sam Toft • Simon James

+ too many musicians to mention…

About the author

APRIL SIMONE

April Simone is an ever-changing colour bursting with love for our Earth and its many occupants. She is devoted to supporting people of all ages, during times of change, challenge and triumph. As she changes and grows, so does her expression of this mission, which can be found at www.aprilsimone.com

www.ingramcontent.com/pod-product-compliance
Lightning Source LLC
Chambersburg PA
CBHW060600080526
44585CB00013B/636